PRAISE
—The Beginner's Guide
Intercessory Prayer

Although this book is called a *Beginner's Guide*, it is really for all prayer warriors, whether just beginning or advanced. This is a fabulous book that will bring the prayer movement to a whole new level of understanding.

Cindy Jacobs
Cofounder, Generals International

I can think of no better author to teach beginning intercessors the keys to intercession than Dutch Sheets. This book is destined to birth a new army of intercessors.

Dick Eastman
International President, Every Home for Christ

Pastor Dutch Sheets is unsurpassed in his God-given ability to help Christians rise to new levels in the ministry of intercession. He has outdone himself in this dynamic new book, and you will not want to miss it!

C. Peter Wagner
President, Global Harvest Ministries

Pastor Dutch weaves in contemporary stories with biblical ones in such a skillful way that one wants to immediately stop and pray. I know I did. How I wish I'd had this book 30 years ago when I wanted to learn the basics on intercessory prayer.

Quin Sherrer
Author, *Lord I Need to Pray with Power*

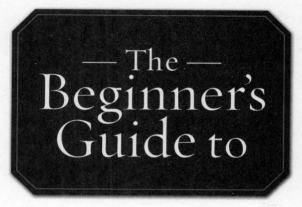

— The — Beginner's Guide to

Intercessory Prayer

DUTCH SHEETS

Regal

From Gospel Light
Ventura, California, U.S.A.

Published by Regal
From Gospel Light
Ventura, California, U.S.A.
www.regalbooks.com
Printed in the U.S.A.

Library of Congress Cataloging-in-Publication Data
Sheets, Dutch.
  The beginner's guide to intercessory prayer / Dutch Sheets
     p. cm.
Includes bibliographical references.
  ISBN 978-08307-4539-5
  1. Intercessory prayer—Christianity. I. Title.
BV210.3.S54 2004
248.3'2—dc22

                                                    2003028095

1 2 3 4 5 6 7 8 9 10 / 10 09 08

Rights for publishing this book outside the U.S.A. or in non-English languages are administered by Gospel Light Worldwide, an international not-for-profit ministry. For additional information, please visit www.glww.org, email info@glww.org, or write to Gospel Light Worldwide, 1957 Eastman Avenue, Ventura, CA 93003, U.S.A.

Contents

Chapter One 7
The Priority of Intercession

Chapter Two 23
The Plan of Intercession

Chapter Three 39
The Person of Intercession

Chapter Four 49
The Purpose of Intercession

Chapter Five 63
The Prize of Intercession

Chapter Six 79
The Place of Intercession

Chapter Seven 91
The Protection of Intercession

Chapter Eight 107
The Power of Intercession

Chapter Nine 125
The Perseverance of Intercession

Chapter Ten 143
Proactive Intercession

Chapter Eleven 161
Proclamation Intercession

Chapter Twelve 175
The Pain of Intercession

Chapter Thirteen 189
The Pleasure of Intercession

Endnotes 197

Bibliography 201

Chapter One

The Priority of Intercession

I recall what it was like when I was courting my wife, Ceci. I was so in love with her that interest in everything else paled in comparison. I thought of her in the morning when I awakened, and she was on my mind when I went to sleep at night.

When we were separated by distance, I was miserable and wrote to her nearly every day. When the time of separation ended and we were together again, I wanted her to always be at my side. Her company was—and remains—my greatest earthly joy.

I like to think of my prayer times as courting God. Sometimes I refer to them as prayer visits—conversing with God as I would with a close family member or friend. I no doubt spend more time doing this than I do making requests. The famous verse in Proverbs that says, "In all your ways acknowledge Him and He will direct your paths" (Prov. 3:6) could be translated, "In all your courting, seek intimacy with Him first." In other words, we are to court God ahead of people, money, success, or any other thing we might seek. As we do, this becomes our greatest motivation for prayer.

The following is a striking example of the motivating power of love:

Alvin Straight, a 73-year-old man from Laurens, Iowa, wanted to visit his 80-year-old brother in Blue River, Wisconsin, who had recently suffered a stroke. The only problem was Alvin didn't have a driver's license due to his poor eyesight. Evidently not willing to take a bus, train, or plane, he had to come up with another solution. Out of determination to see his brother in 1994, Alvin climbed aboard his 1966 John Deere tractor/lawn mower and drove it several hundred miles, a journey of many weeks, to Blue River, Wisconsin.[1]

What a demonstration of the power of love!

Mr. Straight's motivation for such a journey was found in his love for his brother. We, too, are beginning a journey, one of learning to intercede. Our motivation for prayer will also be found in the power of love. As believers in Jesus Christ, we have been invited into a loving relationship with God as Father and Friend. This relationship is *the first priority of intercession*, and our journey must begin here.

All of our Christian endeavors, including prayer, should be born out of intimacy with Him. Paul said to the Corinthians, "But I am afraid, lest as the serpent deceived Eve by his craftiness, your minds should be led astray from the simplicity and purity of devotion to Christ" (2 Cor. 11:3).

Devotion—our relationship with Christ—doesn't need to be complex. Life itself can be a bit overwhelming, and the last thing we need is a complicated walk with God.

Relationship with Jesus must be kept pure and simple. Introducing you to any facet of prayer without making this clear would set you up for frustration and eventual failure. Our motivation for prayer must be relationship—communing with God.

I emphasize this not only because it's true, but also because our human tendencies and needs sometimes cause us to miss this critical starting place in prayer. We are so often "cart before the horse" people. Of the three possible motives and starting points for prayer—communing with God, our needs, and the needs of others—we often begin with the second or third.

However, when Jesus was asked to teach His disciples to pray, He didn't begin with "Our Provider, who art in heaven, generous be Thy name." Nor did He encourage us to start with, "Our Master, who art in heaven, assignment-giver be Thy name." No, Jesus settled the matter once and for all in the only model prayer He ever gave us when He instructed us to begin this way: "Our *Father*" (see Matt. 6:9).

Why is this so important? Because no relationship built around "using" another person becomes lasting and meaningful. On the other hand, loving relationships built around true communion and the pleasure of friendship always result in the serving of one another. Paul said his *love* for God, not duty or reward, constrained him to serve God (see 2 Cor. 5:14, *KJV*).

A wonderful story is told of a couple who shared a great love:

Married for over half a century, this couple played their own special game from the time they met.

The goal was to write "shmily" in a surprise place for the other to find.

"Shmily" was outlined in the sugar and flour, traced in the dew on windows, and written in the steam left on the mirror after a hot shower, where it would reappear bath after bath. At one point, the woman even unrolled an entire roll of toilet paper to leave "shmily" on the very last sheet. Little notes with "shmily" were found on dashboards, car seats, and steering wheels. They were stuffed inside shoes and left under pillows. "Shmily" was written in the dust upon the mantel and traced in the ashes of the fireplace. This mysterious word was as much a part of their house as the furniture.

This couple shared a true love that was pure and enduring. More than just a flirtatious game, their deep love was a way of life whose unmatched beauty could hardly be fathomed. Their relationship was based on a devotion and passionate affection that not everyone experiences. What was the message they shared?

S-h-m-i-l-y: See How Much I Love You.[2]

My daughter Hannah came to me the other day and said, "I love you, Dad."

"Okay, what do you want?" I jokingly replied.

"Nothing," she said. "I just wanted to tell you I love you."

All the emotional bells and whistles went off in my heart. Like any good parent, I love to please my family by providing for them, but nothing compares to being told I'm loved for no other reason than just because I'm loved.

As I jokingly accused Hannah, if our first motivation in prayer is to get our needs met, prayer will simply become a way of "using" God. He will be a convenience, like the store on the corner. Prayer will be a survival technique, a heavenly 9-1-1. This will never result in a consistent, meaningful life of prayer. Just as a human relationship with a "what's in it for me" foundation and motivation will ultimately fail, so too will our relationship with God, if it is founded on such a mindset.

Similarly, if my primary motivation for prayer becomes interceding for others, this, too, will ultimately fail as a motivator. This desire to meet God's need for intercessors, as well as to meet the need others have for intercession, is noble. But whereas the first motivation deteriorates into "using" God, this one will eventually result in a motivation-killing sense of feeling "used." It will lead to a performance-based relationship, or, worse yet, a legalistic religious exercise, neither of which are positive motivators.

If this is our starting point, prayer becomes an *obligation*. We feel like hirelings, working our way to heaven through our sacrificial payment of dues as obedient Christians. This promotes the mistaken belief that the only "well done" we'll ever hear, and the only pleasure we'll ever receive, will be in the "sweet by and by." This is not what our heavenly Father wants. Prayer and intercession should be all about friendship, relationship and partnering with our wonderful Father. Every one of us would rather be a partner than a hired hand.

Jesus, just days before the disciples would receive their greatest commission from Him—"Go into all the world and preach the good news to everyone" (Mark 16:15, *NIV*)—established the working relationship He wanted with them. "I no longer call you servants . . . but friends," He said in John 15:15 (*NIV*).

He reminded His followers that the greatest commandment of God was to love Him, then to love our neighbors as ourselves (see Matt. 22:37-39). This isn't because God is so egotistical and selfish that He just has to be first. Rather, it is to assure us that He wants a loving relationship with us more than He wants our good works. Also, it reminds us that all success and pleasure in life must flow from relationship with our life-giving Creator.

On another occasion, Christ reminded a follower and friend, Martha, that communing with Him was more important than serving Him. While Martha was in the kitchen preparing Him a meal, Mary, her sister, had chosen the more important or, as the *NIV* says, "better" activity of sitting at His feet, listening to Him (see Luke 10:38-42). The following story about a mother busy in her kitchen gives a similar modern-day illustration of this:

> A young mother was trying to get her work done as her little girl, Tracy, watched her. The mother had bread dough on her hands; the daughter had time on her hands. Tracy was out of ideas for entertaining herself and was now relying on her mother for entertainment. The young mother decided to take this opportunity to tell Tracy a Bible story. By doing so, she could continue to knead her bread dough. Her intention was to serve fresh, hot cinnamon bread for dinner. She chose the Bible story of Mary

and Martha as found in Luke 10:38-42. "Mary and Martha and their brother, Lazarus, invited Jesus to their home for dinner," she began as she continued to make cinnamon bread. She looked down and clearly realized that what her daughter really wanted was her undivided attention. She wanted eye-to-eye contact. She wanted her mother to hold her. As she stopped kneading, Tracy looked up at her. "The better part—that's what you want of me, isn't it?" she asked. Tracy nodded.[3]

Oftentimes, we become so focused on completing a specific task that we forget what is really important: to prioritize our relationship with God, first of all, and then with those we love. Through the apostle John, Jesus gently reprimanded the group of believers living in Ephesus (see Rev. 2:1-7). After commending them for their faithfulness and good works, He reminded them that their love relationship with Him was preeminent. They had "left their first love" and were in danger of the inevitable results—disillusionment and lowered motivation. "Remember," I believe He was saying to them, "these good works must flow *out of* relationship with Me, not *define* or *take the place of* it."

Abraham, spoken of in Scripture as a "friend of God" (see 2 Chron. 20:7; Isa. 41:8; Jas. 2:23), was a powerful intercessor, the first intercessor mentioned in the Bible. He wasn't God's friend because he was an intercessor; he was an intercessor because he was God's friend. The difference may be subtle, but I assure you it isn't small. He was quite bold in his intercession, by the way, asking God questions like, "Shall not the judge of all the earth do right?" (see Gen. 18:25).

Intimate relationships produce this kind of boldness: not an arrogant irreverence, but a confident boldness that eliminates the fear of rejection or being misunderstood. When I need a favor, I ask a friend or family member, not a stranger. If it's in that person's power to help me, he or she does. God wants us to be on such intimate terms with Him that it produces bold, confident and effective intercession. I desperately desire that you may experience this type of intimacy in your relationship with God.

Our friendship with God is pictured in the Scriptures by a famous mountain in Israel. Its name, Hebron, actually means "friendship, fellowship, or communion." Abra-ham, God's interceding friend, was associated with this mountain. As an epitaph of sorts, he is buried there with his wife, Sarah. Fittingly, the symbolism associated with this biblical mountain tells us much about friendship with God and what it produces for the intercessor. As you see these wonderful pictures, you, too, will want to live at this "Mountain of Friendship."

First, being *the highest point in Israel, Hebron teaches us that the highlight of the Christian life and the pinnacle from which all else should flow is friendship with the Almighty.* It is only from there, as we look down on all of life, that the correct perspective can be obtained. The psalmist David was confused about the prosperity of wicked people until he saw things from God's point of view:

For I was envious at the foolish, when I saw the prosperity of the wicked. . . . Behold, these are the

ungodly, who prosper in the world; they increase
in riches. . . . When I pondered to understand this,
it was troublesome in my sight (Ps. 73:3,12, *KJV*;
v. 16, *NASB*).

David then went on to explain what eliminated his
confusion:

Until I came into the sanctuary of God; then I
perceived their end. . . . For, behold, those who
are far from Thee will perish; thou hast destroyed
all those who are unfaithful to Thee. But as for
me, the nearness of God is my good; I have made
the Lord God my refuge, that I may tell of all
Thy works (Ps. 73:17,27-28).

Like David, we must take our perspective on life from
God's viewpoint. One of the most important things you'll
learn as God's friend is to intercede from His perspective.
Living at Hebron, the high place of friendship, makes this
possible. As you spend time with God, you'll begin to
think like Him, which will allow you to pray according to
His heart and will. This agreement with God is a key element of intercession, and guarantees success. Many people
spend much of their prayer time asking for their wants,
never thinking about God's heart. Yet, as I have stated,
this isn't true relationship. As you live at Hebron, you will
increasingly care about what is on God's heart, just as He
cares about what is on yours. This partnership is glorious.

Second, Hebron became the home of Caleb, one of the
greatest warriors of Israel. *Friendship with our Father makes*

us powerful overcomers. Caleb, the faith-filled spy and great Israeli conqueror, asked God for Hebron, the "mountain of friendship," as his inheritance. God granted his request, and Hebron, the place of friendship, became the "mountain of the conquering warrior." A warrior heart and a tender heart aren't conflicting. To the contrary, I believe Caleb was a great warrior *because of* his relationship with God. God, your Father and Friend, wants you, also, to be a conquering intercessor living at Hebron. Out of your relationship with Him, you, too, will be a great overcomer.

Ken and Barbara Gaub learned to overcome financial lack through their relationship with God:

Desperately needing a break from their missions work in Kentucky, the Gaubs headed for their parents' home in Washington. Traveling in below-zero weather was challenging—especially with a baby and a partially working car heater. Upon reaching Colorado, they had only a little bit of change left, so Ken pulled into a parking lot to discuss with Barbara what they should do about their critical financial situation.

In amazement Barbara said, "We do what we preach. We believe the Lord and pray." Bowing their heads, they asked the Lord to send help for them. When finished praying, they drove to a service station and sat there, wondering what step to take next.

Another car pulled in behind them, and a lady got out and came up to their window. Very excitedly, she remarked, "I saw you parked back by the grocery store with your heads bowed. I told my husband that I believed you were Christians and that you were praying for financial assistance. I want to help you." Reaching in the window, she placed money in their hands.

Overwhelmed at the miracle they held, they thanked her and praised God for His provision.[4]

This is an example of overcoming through relationship with God. It is a demonstration of faith that God will give us victory in every situation as we partner with Him.

Third, *intimacy with God—living at Hebron—will cause your intercession to defeat the giants in your life and others' lives.* Hebron was formerly ruled by Arba, the greatest of all the giants in the land of Canaan, and had been named after him. Caleb defeated this giant, took the mountain, and renamed it Hebron (see Josh. 14:14-15). Your Father wants you to be an overcoming intercessor, able to defeat every giant that comes your way. Like Caleb, you, too, can live on this mountain representing dead giants, fulfilled destinies, and friendship with God.

Fourth, *a Hebron lifestyle will give you the ability to walk in great authority.* King David was anointed to be king over Judah at Hebron, and he ruled from there for seven years.

Satan, sin, our flesh, and negative circumstances want to rule our lives, but God wants *us* to rule over these things. Romans 5:17 says, "For if by the transgression of the one, death reigned through the one, much more those who receive the abundance of grace and of the gift of righteousness will reign in life through the One, Jesus Christ."

God wants to crown us, like David, with the authority to rule in ungodly situations. Intercessors rule from Hebron.

Through the ministry of intercessor and speaker Quin Sherrer, a mother was awakened to her God-given authority in Christ. She shared the following testimony with Quin:

> When you gave a seminar in our area two years ago, I poured my mother's heart out to you, and you responded by praying for me and my son. When you autographed a copy of your book, you wrote: *"Keep standing in the gap for Steven—a mighty man of valor!"*
>
> At the time, fifteen-year-old Steven was anything but that. He was deeply involved in pornography, drugs, alcohol, the occult, Hell's Angels, the Ku Klux Klan, and organized crime, and was also fascinated with death. God saved Steven the day of his sentencing hearing—the day of his greatest rebellion—when he received three and a half times the sentence he expected. In prison, Steven attended Bible studies, and even though it was extremely difficult, he took a stand for the Lord right where he was. He is now out of prison and planning to attend Bible college.
>
> We knew as we surrendered Steven to the Lord before he was arrested that he would never live at home again. But we stood on Isaiah 54:13 and have seen its fulfillment. Steven is being taught by the Lord, and great is his peace. Yes, God is faithful; He does perform His Word![5]

Quin has learned to reign from Hebron. She taught Suzanne. You, too, will learn to rule from there.

Last, *this great "mountain of friendship" will also become for you a place of refuge.* Hebron became one of the six cities of refuge in Israel, places to which those who accidentally took another's life could run and in which they could live without fear of retribution (see Josh. 20). As you become an intercessor and, more important, one who operates on an intimate basis with God, you'll find this to be a place of great comfort and safety in life.

The following story, which circulated on the Internet, illustrates how concerned intercessors established a place of refuge for hurting children:

> Last school year, an elementary school teacher's classroom was made up of third-graders, every one of whom came from a difficult situation. Some were from single-parent families, some were from dysfunctional families, some were undernourished or uncared for, some lived in abusive homes, and others had been beaten, bruised, or raped by family members. One little girl's dad had died of AIDS, and the list goes on. The teacher's heart bled for these kids.
>
> Before the 1999–2000 school year started, she and her husband went to her classroom and prayed over each desk in the room. *They prayed that God would place an angel behind each and every child throughout the coming year, to watch over them and protect them* [emphasis added].
>
> A month or so after the year started, she gave the kids an assignment to write about what they

would like to be when they grew up. Each was busy with his or her assignment when "Andrew" raised his hand. When she asked him what he needed, he asked her how to spell "mighty." After answering his question, she asked him why he needed to know. Andrew said it was because when he grew up he wanted to be a "mighty man of God." When he said this, little "Mark," sitting next to him, asked, "So, what's a mighty man of God?" The teacher, knowing she could not say anything about this herself in the classroom, told Andrew to go ahead and tell Mark what it was.

Andrew said, "It's a man who puts on the armor of God and is a soldier for God." After observing the conversation between Andrew and Mark, the teacher, with a lump in her throat, had begun to walk away when Andrew motioned with his little forefinger for her to come closer. He whispered to her, asking if she believed in angels. She told him yes, she did. Then he asked her if she thought people could see angels, and she said she thought some people probably could. Andrew said that he did, and he could see an angel standing behind each kid in the room.[6]

This classroom became a place of comfort and safety, a true refuge for these children. God allowed this small child—a mighty man of God in the making—to see the answer to the intercessors' prayers. Their intercession, of course, was born through allowing God's heart for these kids to become their hearts. These are Hebron intercessors, functioning from their places of friendship with God.

God's heart is the same for us as it was for Abraham, Caleb and David. As we learn to become intercessors for Him and with Him, He wants us to do this from Hebron, the place of friendship. The results of this relationship will be fulfillment for both God and us, and victories for many people. Intercession will become a passion, not a performance; a lifestyle, not a labor.

Why don't you pray this important prayer with me?

> *Precious heavenly Father, thank You for telling me in Your Word that You prioritize me above my service. I want to do the same with You—I want to be Your friend. Help me, please, to build this kind of relationship with You. Help me to live at Hebron, enjoying the rest, safety and victory found there. I want to be a giant-killer like David, moving in Your authority and power. I now know that this authority flows from the highest place—friendship with You. Thank You. Amen.*

Did You Understand?

1. What is the first priority of intercession? Can you substantiate this with a few Scripture references?

2. What mountain in Israel pictures our friendship with God? What does this friendship produce, also pictured by this mountain?

3. What are the three possible motives for prayer? Which one must come first? What happens if the others become our first motivation for prayer?

4. You do know, don't you, that you're a worshiping warrior in the making?

Chapter Two

The Plan of Intercession

It was my first baby dedication. I wasn't even pastoring at the time but was serving as a worship leader at Christ for the Nations Institute in Dallas, Texas. The circumstances surrounding this event were special.

"A baby boy was born yesterday and, in the process of the delivery, his skull was fractured by the forceps," was the way the prayer request came to me. "He is the child of an unsaved and unwed mother," the person continued. "Could we pray for him in chapel this morning?"

I felt such compassion, and great faith rose up in me as I boldly led those present in prayer, asking God to heal this child and save this young mother. The incredible testimony came the next day. The child was completely healed and the mother, overwhelmed with God's love, had been led to Christ! Not yet having a home church, she wondered if we at the Bible college would dedicate the baby to Christ, and if the man who had led the prayer—ME!— would do the dedication.

What an exciting day it was! The student body and I rejoiced that God had used us to affect these two precious lives for whom Christ had died. We did not overestimate our part, nor did we underestimate it. We functioned according to *the plan of intercession* and rejoiced with this mother and with heaven at the results.

This story prompts an important question. Did our prayers really cause God to heal this baby and save his mother, or would He have done it anyway, even without our asking? "After all," some would argue, "God is sovereign and all-powerful, isn't He?"

The answer to whether or not God is sovereign is an emphatic "Yes!" But does the fact that He is sovereign mean He operates independently of us humans, always accomplishing His will, regardless of our actions? "NO!" As incredible as it sounds, *a sovereign God made a sovereign choice to limit Himself in many ways and situations to the actions, decisions and requests of human beings*. His plan is to work on Earth with and through us—His family and friends—not independently of us.

Consider the following examples that clearly point out the need for prayer and obedience in order for humans to experience God's will:

- *Healing of a nation*: "If My people, which are called by My name, shall humble themselves, and pray, and seek My face, and turn from their wicked ways; then will I hear from heaven, and will forgive their sin, and will heal their land" (2 Chron. 7:14, *KJV*).

- *Receiving covenantal blessings*: "Now it shall be, if you will diligently obey the Lord your God, being careful to do all His commandments which I command you today, the Lord your God will set you high above all the nations of the earth" (Deut. 28:1; verse 2 and the following verses list several blessings).

- *Experiencing a long life*: "Honor your father and your mother, as the Lord your God has commanded you, that your days may be prolonged, and that it may go well with you in the land which the Lord your God gives you" (Deut. 5:16).

- *Protection from harm*: "He who dwells in the shelter of the Most High will abide in the shadow of the Almighty" (Ps. 91:1).

- *Forgiveness of sin:* "If we confess our sins, He is faithful and righteous to forgive us our sins and to cleanse us from all unrighteousness" (1 John 1:9).

- *The release of God's will on the earth*: "Thy kingdom come. Thy will be done, on earth as it is in heaven" (Matt. 6:10).

John Wesley so believed God's plan was to work on Earth through people that he contended, "God does nothing on the earth save in answer to believing prayer." E. M. Bounds, one whose teachings on prayer have impacted tens of thousands, was just as bold:

God shapes the world by prayer. The more praying there is in the world the better the world will be, the mightier the forces against evil. . . . The prayers of God's saints are the capital stock of heaven by which God carries on His great work upon earth. God conditions the very life and prosperity of His cause on prayer.[1]

Peter Wagner agrees with this when he says:

> We must understand that our sovereign God has for His own reasons so designed this world that much of what is truly His will He makes contingent on the attitudes and actions of human beings. He allows humans to make decisions that can influence history. . . . Human inaction does not *nullify* the atonement, but human inaction can make the atonement *ineffective* for lost people.[2]

As already alluded to, Scripture backs these strong assertions. In 1 Kings 18:1, after three years of drought, God told Elijah He was going to send rain to Israel. Amazingly, even though it was God's will and timing to send the rain, He still needed a human to ask Him. Elijah prayed seven times for the rain to begin before the answer came (see 1 Kings 18:41-45). James 5:17-18 assures us it really was Elijah's prayers that released the rain.

On another occasion, a godly man named Daniel discovered, through the prophecies of Jeremiah, that it was time for the nation of Israel to be restored from its captivity. Again, though it was God's will and timing, Daniel still had to ask (see Dan. 9:3). His prayers generated a great war in the heavens between angels and evil spirits. Through Daniel's persistent prayer, the angels broke through with the answer.

Another powerful example is found in Numbers 14:11-12. God pronounced severe destruction on Israel because of their rebellion. After Moses' intercession, however, He made the incredible announcement, "I have pardoned them according to your word" (Num. 14:20). What an amazing statement! The absolute judge of the universe pardoned according to the words of a human.

In a different situation, God wanted to pardon but couldn't. He said in Ezekiel 22:30-31 that had He found a human to request forgiveness for a certain group of people, He would have spared them from judgment. Listen to these staggering verses:

> "And I searched for a man among them who should build up the wall and stand in the gap before Me for the land, that I should not destroy it; but I found no one. Thus I have poured out My indignation on them; I have consumed them with the fire of My wrath; their way I have brought upon their heads," declares the Lord God.

These and numerous other passages make it clear that God involves Himself in the affairs of Earth through humans, and prayer is one way that He does so. Though the Scriptures assure us God's plans and purposes ultimately will be realized, delays occur at times because He has to wait until He can find people through whom to work. The generation of Israelites that came out of Egyptian slavery missed its destiny; God waited and fulfilled His plans through the next generation. Jesus said Jerusalem in His day missed its time of visitation (see Luke 19:44).

I don't want to cause delays in the purposes of God, and I certainly don't want Him to find someone else to do my part for me. I want to accomplish every part of my

God-given, God-partnering destiny. In the following story, Dr. Ben Carson realized that a successful operation depended not just on his surgical skills, but also on God working through him.

> After nineteen hours of surgery, Dr. Ben Carson and his medical team collapsed, exhausted, into conference room chairs. In the middle of separating two Zambian twins who were born joined at the head, they considered stopping the operation. But as dangerous as it looked to proceed, it would, in effect, be a death sentence if they stopped.
>
> As they walked back to the operating room, Dr. Carson prayed that God would take over the operation. As he resumed the delicate surgery in the South African hospital, struggling with just a scalpel instead of the microinstruments he used at home, he sensed a remarkable steadiness in his hands. It was as though he were simply watching his hands move, while someone else had actually taken over the surgery. While he had often sensed prayer support during other surgeries, he had never experienced anything like what happened during this intricate operation. At the very moment that the last vein connecting the boys was separated, the stereo system began playing "Hallelujah Chorus," from Handel's *Messiah*. Everyone in the OR knew something remarkable had taken place. The twenty-eight-hour surgery was a complete success, and the boys fully recovered at an astonishing rate.[3]

Dr. Carson recognized his inability to complete this operation on his own. God heard his request, and as He worked through him, these boys received restoration, healing and wholeness. This is a beautiful example of God and humans working together through both prayer and action.

Let's back up to God's original intent to work on Earth through us and see if we can understand it further. The name Adam means "man" or "humankind." God made a man and called him "man"—Adam. In fact, often in Scripture the generic term "man" is the Hebrew word *adam*. As the first human, he represents all of us. What God intended for Adam, He intended for the entire human race.

When God created Adam and Eve, He made them His *governors* or *managers* of the earth. Psalm 8:6 says of Adam, "Thou dost make him to rule over the works of Thy hands; Thou hast put all things under his feet." The word "rule" is translated from the Hebrew word that means "manager, steward, or governor."[4] God's intent was for "adams"—humankind—to govern the earth as His representatives. Notice that I didn't say instead of Him, but rather as His representatives. Humanity was to do it under His authority, principles and direction.

Psalm 115:16 confirms this: "The heavens are the heavens of the Lord; but the earth He has given to the sons of men." James Moffat translates the last part of this verse, "the earth *He has assigned to men*" (emphasis added), which communicates with greater accuracy the meaning of the Hebrew word translated "given."[5] God didn't give away *ownership* of the earth, but He did assign to humanity *the responsibility of governing it.*

Genesis 2:15 says, "Then the Lord God took the man and put him into the garden of Eden to cultivate it and keep it." The word "keep" comes from a Hebrew word that also means "to guard or protect."[6] It is the primary word used for a watchman in the Scriptures. Adam literally was God's watchman or guardian on the earth.

So literal and final was God's decision to rule the earth through adams (or humans) that the first adam had the ability and power to give this authority to another—Satan. Luke 4:6-7 says, "And the devil said to Him, 'I will give You all this domain and its glory; for it has been handed over to me, and I give it to whomever I wish. Therefore if You worship before me, it shall all be Yours.'" Jesus actually referred to Satan as "the ruler of this world" three times in the Gospels (see John 12:31; 14:30; 16:11).

Consistent with God's original plan, so complete was His decision to work on the earth through people that, in order to reverse this situation, Jesus had to become human! He had to become an adam (see 1 Cor. 15:45). *Humans were forever to be God's link to authority and activity on the earth.* We were to be His mediators or representatives. God's *plan of intercession* is to work on the earth with and through us, not independently of us. He honors this decision in every way. Even the incredible task of spreading the Good News of salvation requires our involvement. Romans 10:13-15 asks several rhetorical questions, the implied answer to each being "They will not."

For whoever will call upon the name of the Lord will be saved. How then shall they call upon Him in whom they have not believed? And how shall they believe in Him whom they have not heard? And how shall they hear without a preacher? And how shall they preach unless they are sent?

The entire story of the Bible is one of God and humans working together on the earth. As our biblical examples have shown, God finds a human to act *for* Him or ask *of* Him, which involves Him in situations. Consider these additional verses:

- He instructs us to ask for His kingdom to come, His will to be done (see Matt. 6:10). Surely He wouldn't want us to waste our time asking for something that was going to happen anyway, would He?

- He instructs us to ask for our daily bread (see Matt. 6:11). Yet, He knows our needs before we even ask.

- He instructs us to ask that laborers be sent into the harvest (see Matt. 9:38). Yet, doesn't the Lord of the harvest want that more than we do?

- Paul said, "Pray for us that the word of the Lord may spread rapidly and be glorified" (2 Thess. 3:1). Wasn't God already planning to distribute His word among the people?

Are not these things God's will? Why, then, are we supposed to ask Him for something He already wants to do, if it's not that our asking somehow releases Him to do it?

Notice that nowhere in the Bible does God instruct us to ask for things that are going to happen automatically. He never tells us to ask for the sun to shine, for air to breathe, or for gravity to perform its work. He only tells us to ask for things He has made contingent on us. He is so determined to work through our prayers, He has said it is possible to "have not because we ask not" (see Jas. 4:2). Though there are certainly sometimes reasons for unanswered prayer, this verse tells us there are times when the reason we do not get what we want is simply that we didn't ask for it.

Quin Sherrer shares the miraculous story of what happened when a mother realized she needed to specifically request God to touch her son.

God cares about even the small details of our lives. Eleanor was a Christian who knew God cared, but she had a child with a very special need. Would God really intervene? After hearing me speak on prayer at a meeting in Alabama, Eleanor realized three things: she hadn't been giving God quality time; she hadn't been praying with definite requests; and she had never really let God speak to her through His Word.

She left that meeting with a burning desire to pray, and with a definite plan for how to do it.

The problem: Eugene, her thirteen-year-old adopted son, had not grown even an eighth of an inch in a year. At first she thought it was just his Asian heritage; then her doctor told her to take him to a specialist who would prescribe growth hormones.

The plan: Eleanor's habit for years had been to rise at 4:30 A.M. and run for several miles. Then she usually came home, flopped down to rest, and said about ten minutes worth of general "God-bless-us" prayers.

"I realized the time I spent with the Lord was like 'snack time,' when 'banquet time' was what I really needed," she said. "I decided to start praying first; then if I had any time left, I'd run."

During one of her first mornings of spending quality time with God, He showed her a specific Scripture verse she could pray for her son. She paraphrased it: "Lord, may my son, like Jesus, increase in wisdom and stature and favor with God and man" (see Luke 2:52, *KJV*).

She never got around to taking Eugene for the hormone shots. He began to grow. In the first three months after she started praying this way, he grew three inches! In the next three months, he grew three more. Some people may argue that it was his natural growth-spurt year, but Eleanor is convinced God honored her prayer. She saw other evidence of answered prayer. Her son's conduct grade on his report card went from a C- to an A. "Mom, my teacher likes me now, and I like her," he commented when she quizzed him about it.

"Eugene increased not only in stature and favor with his teacher, but in wisdom, too, as his other grades also have improved," Eleanor told me when I saw her months later. "Sometimes he laughs and says, 'Mom, I can't get away with anything anymore, because God always shows you when I've done something wrong.' But he's very interested to know what Scriptures I'm praying for him, and he is glad I'm praying so specifically.

"I still take time to run after my prayer time," she added, smiling. "But I find it more invigorating after coming directly from my prayer closet."[7]

This brings us to a very important word in our understanding of intercession: _representation_. It comes from a Latin word meaning "to present again." As intercessors we re-present, or present again, the needs of another to the Father in heaven.

This is a dual representation. As we do this, not only are we representing the person with the need, we are also representing Christ. We are His ambassadors on the earth, those through whom He wants His love and redemption represented to the human race. Second Corinthians 5:20 tells us, "Therefore, we are ambassadors for Christ, as though God were entreating through us; we beg you on behalf of Christ, be reconciled to God." These two facets of representation—presenting someone's need to the Father and doing this through the work of Christ—are _the plan of intercession._

As I shared in _Intercessory Prayer_, my first book on prayer, the Lord made this real to me several years ago on a missions trip to Guatemala. I had traveled with a team to a remote village, far from any modern city. There was no electrical power, no plumbing, no phones. Our purpose in being there was to build shelters for the villagers whose adobe homes had been destroyed in the devastating earthquake of 1976. It had killed thirty thousand people and left one million homeless. We had trucked in materials and were building small, one-room homes for the villagers during the daylight hours. In the evenings we would hold services in the center of the village, preaching the gospel of Jesus Christ to them, explaining that His love was motivating us to spend our time, money and energies helping them. In other words, *we were representing Christ.*

We had been ministering for one week, with very few people coming to Christ. The people were listening, but not responding. I was to preach on the final night of our trip. Just as the service was about to begin, a team member told me about something he and others had found on the far side of the village—a little girl, six or seven years old, tied to a tree.

Not believing what they were seeing, they asked the family that lived there, "Why is this small girl tied to that tree?" It was obvious she lived there, much like a dog, in the back yard—nasty, filthy, helpless and alone.

"She is crazy," the parents replied. "We can't control her. She hurts herself and others and runs away if we turn her loose. There is nothing else we can do for her, so we just have to tie her up."

My heart broke as the team member shared what he had seen. It was on my mind as we began the service. A few minutes into my message, standing on a folding table under the stars, the same God who had asked me to represent Him in Guatemala began speaking to me again.

Tell them you are going to pray for the little insane girl across the village tied to the tree (representing her to the Father). *Tell them you are going to do it in the name of this Jesus you've been preaching about* (representing Christ). *Tell them that through Him you are going to break the evil powers controlling her—that when she is free and normal, they can then know that what you are preaching is true. They can believe that the Jesus you are preaching about is who you say He is. Represent, son, represent!*

With fear and trembling, I began informing the people about what I was planning to do. (I'm a human representative just like you and sometimes representing God can be intimidating.) They nodded in recognition as I mentioned the girl. Expressions of intrigue turned to astonishment as they listened to my plans.

Then I prayed.

On a moonlit night in a tiny, remote village of Guatemala with a handful of people as my audience, my life changed forever. I was about to truly experience the meaning of being Christ's representative on the earth.

Jesus came out of hiding. He became alive: relevant . . . sufficient . . . available! A "hidden" Jesus emerged from the cobwebs of theology. A yesterday Jesus became a today and forever Jesus. A Galilee Jesus became a Guatemala Jesus.

And a new plan unfolded to me. A new concept emerged—Jesus and me. For the first time I truly understood the heavenly pattern: God and me working together. A mere mortal—a human—becoming a conduit for the power of God on Earth. The provision of the cross flowing through a person . . . an earthling. God's infiniteness somehow manifesting through my finiteness. In a simple prayer, I presented the needs of the girl to the Father. I also presented the finished work of Christ in her behalf.

Yes, He set the little girl free.

Yes, the village turned to Christ.

Yes, Jesus prevailed through one of His representatives—an intercessor—on Earth.

As unusual as this story is, I want you to understand that it is not God's *exception* to use us—we are the *plan*. He wants us to approach His throne "boldly," confident of that plan and confident of the relationship. You can do this. As you read this book, you will become equipped to do so. You'll understand the plan.

Let's continue the journey . . . exciting things are ahead of us.

Let's pray this prayer together:

Father, it is amazing how much You have desired to partner with me. Help me to embrace the incredible privilege of representing You on Earth. I want to be a prayer ambassador of heaven. Teach me Your ways, that I might walk in Your plan of intercession effectively. "May Your kingdom come and Your will be done" is my fervent prayer. Amen.

Did You Understand?

1. Is God all-powerful? Does this mean that He operates independently of humans? How does this relate to prayer?

2. Can you give biblical examples of God using people to accomplish His will?

3. Can you give a biblical example of God's will not being accomplished because He could not find an intercessor?

4. Can you explain what it means to "represent" God?

5. Has your Jesus come out of hiding?

Chapter Three

The Person of Intercession

Orlando, Florida, June 2000.

I'm sitting in Orlando, Florida, at Wet & Wild—though I am neither—soaking up the shade and practicing the important discipline of keeping my mind on things that are pure. I have the privilege and important responsibility of guarding the table, chairs and umbrella we snagged. I paid $30 for this privilege—a real bargain.

I use the word "privilege" because this is right where I want to be—in the shade. I'm not a sunbather. I don't like the greasy sunscreens, the heat or the sweat—and that pretty much covers this ridiculous practice.

I'm not really a water person either. I believe God made water for drinking, bathing and fishing (not necessarily in that order). Even Christ had the foresight to choose fishermen who owned a boat as some of His first followers. Notice that He didn't choose skiers, divers, swimmers or sunbathers.

Back to my privilege and responsibility. I chose the words "important responsibility" because that's exactly what my assignment is. Chairs and umbrellas at Wet & Wild are worth somewhere around $1,000 a day, give or take a few dollars. Elsewhere, you could purchase these cheap plastic items for under $100, but here they're *worth* much more because only one set is available for every ten thousand families. One guy just offered me $500 for mine; I laughed at him.

I have counted the cost of this assignment. I'm ready to defend my treasure at the risk of pain and suffering. *No one* is getting my shade. One big body-builder guy threatened to kick sand in my face if I didn't give up these treasures. Luckily for him, a security guy came along right then and whisked him away. He could have been seriously hurt.

While sitting in the shade, I've thought a time or two about Scriptures like "turning the other cheek," "give and it shall be given to you" and "if someone asks for your shirt, give them your coat also." After deciding these verses don't apply to this situation, I'm rejoicing that Jesus didn't say, "If someone takes your chairs at Wet & Wild, give them your umbrella, also." After all, I want to remain pure while fulfilling this assignment.

Actually, casting aside my frivolous jargon, there have been some truly spiritual moments associated with this day. When I'm at places such as this with lots of people, I often find myself observing, thinking and sometimes praying for those I see.

Invariably, I find myself contemplating the lostness of those around me. If you look past the façades, you can see the truth in their actions, if not in their eyes and faces:

- a young girl flaunting her body, looking for love and acceptance
- a man's roaming, lust-filled eyes, looking for pleasure and someone else to conquer

- a group of teenagers playing the "who can be coolest" game, striving for a sense of worth and self-identity
- a macho, domineering father and husband, needing the feeling of power
- the person all alone, looking for someone to come along and fill the aching need for companionship
- the boozer who long ago decided a temporary, drug-induced high was better than no high at all

They don't know it, but they're all looking for the same thing—the fulfillment, peace and self-identity that can be found only one way—through a meaningful relationship with their Creator, Jesus Christ. Acts 4:12 tells us, "There is no other name under heaven that has been given among men, by which we must be saved."

This word "saved" means so much more than a ticket to heaven. It means wholeness, well-being, soundness and peace—things we humans crave that are found only in the Person of Jesus Christ. There is no other name given among men by which we find them.

This is the reason why I prayed here at Wet & Wild, and it's also why I want you to be an intercessor. Your prayers and mine can make a difference. We must become convinced of this. Our prayers can be *irresistible* to God and *indefensible* to Satan. That's pretty strong language, isn't it? Do I believe it? Yes, and so can you.

Back in my study, Colorado Springs, Colorado
I recently listened to a Denver, Colorado, radio talk-show host state his conviction that prayer really didn't motivate

God to do things. "God doesn't answer prayer," he postu-
lated. "Its benefit is simply to help us emotionally." What a
waste of time! A bottle of whiskey can accomplish that, at
least for a few hours. So can pleasures, money, even tantrums.
I prefer to believe what the Bible says about prayer: "Ask, and
it shall be given to you" (Matt. 7:7).

What is the key to such faith? What can make us confident difference-makers in intercessory prayer? The answer
is found in understanding *the Person of intercession*. Chapters
1 and 2 showed us the *priority* of relationship with God and
His *plan* of working through humans. In this chapter we
will define intercession and learn that it flows through a *Person*, Jesus Christ. Our *prayers* of intercession must be offered
through the *Person* of intercession.

When Christ instructed us to ask the Father in His name,
He wasn't giving us a formula but rather describing *a legal
premise* for asking. Consider the following verses:

- John 14:6: "Jesus said to him, 'I am the way, and the
  truth, and the life; no one comes to the Father, but
  through Me.'"
- Hebrews 10:19: "Therefore, brethren, we have confidence to enter the holy place by the blood of Jesus."
- 1 John 2:1: "And if anyone sins, we have an Advocate
  with the Father, Jesus Christ the righteous."
- 1 Timothy 2:5: "There is one God, and one media-
  tor also between God and men, the man Christ Jesus."

In these, and numerous other verses, God is telling us,
"If you want something from Me, there is only one way I can
give it to you—on the basis of what My Son has accom-

plished." He operates on this premise, not because He is a legalistic, narrow-minded dictator—"it's My way or the highway"—or because He is an arrogant parent insisting that His Son take center stage. He demands this approach to Him because only through the legal sacrifice of Christ as our substitute can we enter into relationship with Him and partake of the privileges such a relationship provides. It is impossible for Him to relate to us any other way.

When we understand this truth and pray "in Jesus' name," we come before the Judge of the universe on the proper legal grounds: through the finished work of Christ. We're saying, in essence, "Father, I don't come to You based on my own worthiness, or on the worthiness of the person for whom I'm praying. I come to You on the merits of Your Son, Jesus, and the blood He shed. I am asking *in His name*." The Father responds because His Son, the cross, and Christ's passionate love for us are *irresistible* to Him.

In Acts 3, Peter was used to heal a lame man who had been in that condition for 40 years. The man was so well-known and the miracle so profound that all Jerusalem was amazed (see Acts 3:1-10). When questioned about how this miracle took place, Peter's response was, "On the basis of faith *in His name, it is the name of Jesus* which has strengthened this man whom you see and know; and the faith which comes through Him has given him this perfect health in the presence of you all" (v. 16).

I witnessed a similar healing in my brother Tim's church in Middletown, Ohio. Through a mistake during back surgery, a young man had become paralyzed on one side of his body. He, his family, my brother, and his church had been asking God to heal him.

On a Sunday morning, as Tim again prayed for this young man *in the name of Jesus*, God answered the prayer. It was electrifying! The power of God went through his body and completely healed him of all paralysis. He began to run around the large church as holy pandemonium reigned in the meeting. Friends and family members ran to embrace him and to join the celebration.

Don't let anyone tell you Jesus doesn't heal today.

What about our prayers being indefensible to Satan? When Christ made the great declaration on the cross, "It is finished" (John 19:30), He wasn't announcing His death. The word He spoke was the Greek word used in the markets for "paid in full."[1] He was saying, "I have paid the legal penalty and debt of the human race for their sin and disobedience to God. Every person can now go free from Satan's dominance and oppression." No wonder rocks split, the earth quaked, and the veil of the Temple was torn in two when Christ made this thunderous declaration (see Matt. 27:50-54).

Expounding on this, the Scriptures state in 1 John 3:8, "The Son of God appeared for this purpose, that He might destroy the works of the devil." "Destroy" is a legal word that means "to pronounce or determine that something or someone is no longer bound; that which was legally binding is no longer."[2] Christ was announcing that the human race was free from the legal bondage of Satan.

Satan, of course, knows this, but he is skillful at keeping people ignorant of it, in order to prevent them from believing in the finished work and accepting the results.

However, it is true nonetheless. Our job as intercessors is to enforce this victory in prayer, *through the name of Jesus*. Throughout this book, we will see different facets of how to do this. At this point in our journey, however, our goal is simply to understand that the legal foundation of intercession is Jesus.

A friend of mine once prayed for a lady who was paralyzed from the neck down. Her pastor informed him that she had been that way for two years but that the doctors could find no medical reason. My friend was prompted by the Holy Spirit that the cause was demonic, so he knelt beside her wheelchair and prayed, "Satan, I break your hold over this young lady *in the name of Jesus*. I command you to loose your hold over her and let her go." He was announcing that she was no longer bound and declaring that the debt for her freedom was paid in full.

No immediate change occurred, but a week later she began to move slightly. Her recovery steadily continued and, within a month, she was totally healed, freed from the paralysis that had bound her. That is understanding *the Person of intercession* and enforcing the victory of Calvary.

In chapter 2, we saw why we must ask the Father for those benefits Christ has provided—both for ourselves and for others—even though it is a finished work. Our asking, however, will be anemic if not rooted in the truth of this chapter: God's plan for redeeming people is found in a Person—His Son, Jesus Christ. Our *prayers* of intercession must flow through Him and the power He released at the cross.

Perhaps you have noticed that I have not yet provided a succinct definition of intercessory prayer. That is not an oversight on my part. Succinct definitions are not as important as understanding concepts and principles. In fact, it can be dangerous to formulize or too narrowly define spiritual truth.

Actually, all that I have shared with you thus far has been a definition of intercessory prayer:

- It is born of relationship with God.
- It is necessary because of, and to fulfill, our assignments of governing, managing and stewarding the earth for God.
- It is a representing (re-presenting) of God's will and provision to humankind and of humankind's needs to God.
- It must be done through Christ, in His name.
- It enforces Christ's victory at Calvary.

Added to this list could be all the practical applications to be found in the following chapters. Not only will they reveal many of the how-tos and who-fors, but they will also bring added enlightenment about what intercessory prayer really is.

We're making good progress. Our bags are packed, we have the necessary basics, and our journey toward becoming effective intercessors is well underway. Now, let's move on into our destinies!

Let's pray this prayer together:

Father, I now know I must come to You in the name of Your Son, Jesus. Help me to understand this fully. Make me a world-changer, a difference-maker, a liberator,

*an intercessor who knows how to pray according to the
pattern. Help me to understand the work of Christ.
Give me Your heart for the broken, the hurting, and the
lost. Help me to see them through Your passionate eyes.
I ask this, of course, in Jesus' name.
Amen.*

Did You Understand?

1. What does it mean to pray "in Jesus' name"?
   How does this move the heart of God, our
   Father?

2. What does the phrase "It is finished" mean?
   How did this impact Satan?

3. What do the Scriptures mean when they say
   Jesus destroyed the works of the devil?

Chapter Four

The Purpose of Intercession

I stared with wonder at the awesome splendor of the sunset on the horizon, splashing its mix of orange hues across the majestic mountaintops. What can compare with a sunset in the Rockies? Wonderment set in again as I remembered that I was gazing at a picture of two things very important to God and to us: *destiny* and *intercessory prayer*.

One of the New Testament words for "destiny" is *horizo*. In this Greek word, it is easy to see the English word "horizon," which is the point where the earth and the sky meet. *Horizo* also means a boundary, because the concept of a horizon involves the farthest limits of sight. It doesn't take much imagination to see the concept of destiny in this word. Our destiny is our God-given horizon or boundary. God has predetermined the *boundaries* or *horizons* of our lives. He has "predestined" the plans and purposes He has for each of us, before we were even born.[1]

Psalm 139:15-16 confirms this great truth:

My frame was not hidden from Thee, when I was made in secret, and skillfully wrought in the depths of the earth. Thine eyes have seen my unformed substance; and in Thy book they were all written, the days that were ordained for me, when as yet there was not one of them.

Jeremiah 29:11 tells us, " 'For I know the plans that I have for you,' declares the Lord, 'plans for welfare and not for calamity, to give you a future and a hope.' " The next time you gaze out at the horizon, let it remind you that God has a destiny for you.

I hope your "wheels" are now turning with the question, "But how are horizons and destinies connected to intercession?" The answer is simple: Like the horizon, intercession involves a meeting of heaven and Earth, and there destinies are shaped.

Jesus spoke of heaven meeting Earth when He exhorted us to pray, "Thy will be done on earth as it is in heaven" (Matt. 6:10). Christ was revealing that the God-ordained purpose of prayer is the connecting of heaven and Earth, allowing Him to marry the two, making His plans, purposes and destinies a reality in the hearts of people.

Jesus said prayer would cause heaven and Earth to meet and, consistent with this, the Hebrew word for "intercession," *paga*, actually means "a meeting" or "to meet with."[2] The word isn't always used in the context of prayer—any meeting can be a *paga*—but where prayer is concerned, heaven and Earth meet when we *paga* (intercede). Destinies are released, glorious horizons are revealed, and the Son shines through.

This is *the purpose of intercession: creating meetings*. We meet with God (prayer meetings are appropriately named), and through this meeting He meets with others. One meeting leads to another. Because God is so relational, it shouldn't surprise us that "to meet with" is one of the fundamental meanings of the word *paga*.

Although the word "intercession" has come to be synonymous with "prayer" in our minds, and it is a type of prayer, this Hebrew word for "intercession"—*paga*—does not necessarily mean prayer at all. It has many shades of meaning, all of which can be accomplished through prayer. We will discuss several of these meanings in the following chapters and apply them to intercessory prayer.

If we miss the God of meetings, we miss the God of the Bible.

- He met with Adam and Eve in the cool of the day to commune with them.
- He met with Abraham in order to covenant with him and become his friend.
- He met with Moses on the mountain and in the tabernacle to impart wisdom for leading a nation.
- He met with David on the hills around Bethlehem to make him a lion, bear, and giant killer, and to put in him the qualities of a king.
- He met with Mary to make her the mother of God.
- He met with many sick and diseased people to heal their bodies.
- He met with the 12 to shape them into apostles.
- He met with the 120 in the upper room to make them "little Christs," which is the meaning of the word "Christians."

Everything changes when people meet with God. An immoral woman with five failed marriages became an evangelist of sorts after an encounter with Christ (see John 4). She was so excited about the meeting that she ran back to her city and said, "Come, see a man who told me all the things that I have done; this is not the Christ, is it?"

(v. 29). Jesus was so excited that He lost His appetite. "I'd rather meet than eat," He said (my interpretation of v. 34).

A Jewish zealot, Saul, famous for his persecution of the Church, met the Lord on a road to Damascus. It was a rather unpleasant meeting, with pleasant results. Saul found himself licking the dust at the feet of the Christ he was persecuting, and was blinded for three days by the brightness of His glory (see Acts 9:1-9). As a result of the meeting, Saul decided, "If you can't beat Him, join Him." He was beaten by the meetin'! He later became the apostle Paul. God meetings are powerful!

> One powerful meeting occurred in an Ethiopian hospital where a Muslim sheik, Mohammed Amin, was confined to bed. Diagnosed with AIDS, his weight had dropped to eighty pounds. Without hope, the doctors told him he was about to die.
>
> Then some Christians prayed for him. Mohammed had a vision, and Jesus told him to rise up, live, and serve Him. Mohammed became a Christian at that moment, and his body was healed. At his checkup a month later, medical personnel were shocked to find he was completely free of AIDS.
>
> Since beginning his ministry as a Christian evangelist, he has led thousands of Muslims to Christ. In Woldya, Mohammed led a Muslim family to Christ. Within two years, more than seven hundred Muslims had become Christians. A few years ago, the village of Orgo had no Christians.

Now, after Mohammed's evangelism, there are over four hundred Muslim converts there.

Mohammed's ministry has faced many difficulties. He's been beaten, jailed, and threatened with death. Yet, trusting in God's protection, he declares his outreach to Ethiopian Muslims will continue. "I believe God is going to keep me for many years to come," says Mohammed, "and I give glory to God for everything."[3]

In order to fully understand the purpose of intercession—meetings—it is helpful to see this purpose in the context of man's great need to be reconciled or reconnected to God after the Fall. Job stated the condition of every human being when he cried, "For He is not a man as I am that I may answer Him, that we may go to court together. There is no umpire between us, who may lay his hand upon us both" (Job 9:32-33). Again, in Job 23:3, he said, "Oh that I knew where I might find Him, that I might come to His seat!" Job's destiny was marred. He couldn't find the destiny-writer. His horizon was clouded.

Sin had separated the human race from God. God immediately began the process of reconnecting us to Him and to our divine destinies. He gave Moses plans for a tabernacle and a sacrificial system that would temporarily cover Israel's sins, allowing them to meet with Him. After giving these instructions in Exodus, He told Moses, "I will meet there with the sons of Israel, and it shall be consecrated by My glory" (Exod. 29:43). Again, in verse 45, He states, "I will dwell among the sons of Israel and will be their God." God's heart has always been to meet with

His beloved creation, as these verses so clearly reveal.

All of the Old Testament sacrificial system was temporary, however, until the ultimate sacrifice of Christ on the cross. He was to become the final sacrifice that would do more than cover our sins and allow sporadic meetings in tabernacles and temples. God's ultimate plan was to fully reconnect us, making us His very temple again: "But the one who joins himself to the Lord is one spirit with Him. Or do you not know that your body is a temple of the Holy Spirit who is in you?" (1 Cor. 6:17,19).

This, of course, happens through Christ, who became our reconnector:

> Therefore if any man is in Christ, he is a new creature; the old things passed away; behold, new things have come. Now all these things are from God, who reconciled us to Himself through Christ. . . . God was in Christ reconciling the world to Himself, not counting their trespasses against them (2 Cor. 5:17-19).

Yet God's amazing plan doesn't end there with Christ the Reconciler. As members of the family, He has brought us into this wonderful plan of reconciling the world to Himself. He wants to meet—reconnect—with other people through us. These same verses tell us we share Christ's ministry of reconciling: "[He] gave us the ministry of reconciliation. . . . He has committed to us the word of reconciliation" (2 Cor. 5:18-19).

Our part in this ministry of reconciliation takes place in various ways: through sharing the gospel (which means "good news") with people, by helping to send and support others who spread the gospel, and certainly through intercessory prayer. Webster defines intercession as: "to act *between* parties with a view to *reconcile* those who differ."[4] In intercessory prayer we place ourselves between another person and God, becoming the reconciling link. When for any reason we meet with God for another, becoming the reconciling link between the two, intercession has occurred. It might be for salvation, deliverance, healing, financial provision—any human need.

Though much of this and the next chapter focus primarily on the salvation of the lost, I have seen meetings occur between God and humans for just about any purpose imaginable. I recall seeing the healing of a young boy with a deformed leg. After prayer, he took off his brace, looked in astonishment at his now-normal leg, and proceeded to run for the first time in his life. That was a meeting!

Gordon Lindsay, founder of Christ for the Nations in Dallas, Texas, and one used mightily in healing meetings, told of the dramatic healing of a U.S. congressman:

> Congressman William D. Upshaw from Georgia served four terms in Congress. An unusually gifted speaker, his name was known by millions of people. As a Christian, he was once vice-president of the Southern Baptist Convention, and his reputation for integrity was unquestioned. At the age of eighteen, he severely injured his spine, and he was a total invalid for seven years. By sheer determination, he finally was able to move about with

crutches, although painfully. Many people were aware of the congressman's affliction, with which he suffered for sixty-six years. In 1951, he was miraculously healed in front of an audience of two thousand people. At the command of the man who prayed for the sick, Congressman Upshaw threw away his crutches and ran! He returned to visit his friends in Congress and testified of the great things the Lord had done for him. He often amazed his old friends by walking in upon them as briskly as a young man. Speaking of his remarkable deliverance, he said, "I laid aside my crutches and started toward my happy, shouting wife . . . and the bottom of heaven fell out. Heaven came down our souls to greet, and glory crowned the mercy seat!"[5]

I'd say that qualifies as a meeting! As wonderful as healing "meetings" are, even greater is the healing of the spirit when a person receives salvation. Back in the 1970s, my brother, Tim, and I worked in the same concrete construction company. As every believer in Christ should, we prayed for our coworkers and looked for ways to share Christ with them. We realized He wanted to connect with them through us.

We particularly targeted certain individuals, one of whom was a young man I'll call Bob. Bob seemed fairly open and had lots of questions. Having come from an unchurched and somewhat rough past, he, like many folks, was into alcohol and drugs and was very proficient at profanity. Generally speaking, he was quite adept at sinning.

I learned a long time ago, however, that God loves sinners. No, He doesn't like sin. But unlike many Christians, He doesn't allow that to destroy His love for the person. He actually allowed a prostitute to wash His feet with her tears and hair on one occasion, right in front of several religious leaders (see Luke 7:38). I'm not as secure as He was—that would have made me very uncomfortable. Jesus, on the other hand, saw it as a chance to meet, not retreat.

Back to Bob . . . we spoke much to him about the Lord and prayed for him regularly. Finally, the day came when he was open and interested enough to attend a service with us. We were part of a Christian band, and Bob agreed to come hear us.

In the meeting that night, Bob had a meeting of his own. Christ met him at his personal well of despair (like the immoral woman), interrupted his destructive journey with His glorious light of truth (like Saul), connected heaven and Earth, and reconciled him to God. Another destiny was being formed. Prayer meetings had allowed the God of meetings to meet with another searching soul . . . and He had used us to do it!

What a night! The fruit of intercession! As He did with Bob, Jesus wants to have encounters with people today through our intercession. We're His link. Our prayers release the fruit of Calvary.

Intercession plays a vital role, not only in preparing the sinner but also in the sending of laborers into the harvest. As recorded in Matthew 9:38 (*NKJV*), Jesus said that more laborers were needed for the harvesting of souls. "Therefore," He said, "pray the Lord of the harvest to *send* out laborers." He was saying in essence, "I want to meet with more people in order to reconcile them to the Father. We need more laborers to accomplish this, but you must ask in order for them to be sent."

When Paul and Barnabas were sent into the harvest in Acts 13, they were sent by prayer. "Then, when they had fasted and prayed and laid their hands on them, they *sent them away*" (Acts 13:3, emphasis added). We tend to first think of money when we speak of sending laborers, as our focus is usually on the financial support needed, but neither of these two passages even mentions it. Jesus said, and the Early Church believed, that prayer is the greatest necessity in sending reconciling laborers.

Not only do we send these harvesters forth with prayer, but intercession also opens doors for them to share the gospel and enables them to communicate it with greater skill. Paul said in Colossians 4:2-4 (emphasis added):

> Devote yourselves to prayer, keeping alert in it with an attitude of thanksgiving; praying at the same time for us as well, *that God may open up to us a door for the word,* so that we may speak forth the mystery of Christ, for which I have also been imprisoned; *in order that I may make it clear in the way I ought to speak.*

Paul understood not only that he was sent by prayer, but also that his success at all stages of the harvesting process was dependent on prayer! Intercessory prayer makes possible the ministry of reconciliation—meetings with God.

Susan Morin was a reconciler, a meeting-creator and an intercessor. She joined heaven and Earth, impacting destinies:

Wanting to do something for God, Susan committed to pray during her forty-five-minute daily commute and asked God for whom she should pray. A note at work caught her attention. "I'm sorry this payment is late. I have been seriously ill. Thank you, Beverly." Susan knew she was to pray for her, but not knowing any details, it was difficult. As she faithfully interceded, however, God's great love for Beverly was imparted to her. Susan sent her cards, explaining how God loved her and had led Susan to pray. No responses came, but Susan continued praying.

Nine months later, Beverly's husband called. Having found Susan's well-worn cards, which evidently meant a lot to his wife, he wanted to share what had happened. Although diagnosed with lung cancer, Beverly had never experienced any pain. Church had never had any real part in their lives, but two weeks before she died, Beverly had asked to be baptized. The night before she died, she told him it was OK; she was going home to be with her Lord.

Susan was overwhelmed that God had used her to reveal His love to Beverly, allowing Him to meet with her and reconcile her to Himself.[6]

The world is filled with hurting Beverlys, desperately longing for someone to care. Somewhere along their journeys, storm clouds blew in, blocking the glorious "Sonsets" God had planned for them. Each has a name; each has a story. God knows every one of them, from the career-minded yuppie to the homeless, orphaned child feeding on garbage.

Somehow, we must find the heart to care. Jesus desperately needs us to fulfill our part in the reconciliation process. Don't be deceived into thinking you can't make a difference. Like Susan, your commute can become a communing, and the miles can become meetings.

Please, for the passion of the Son, and for the Beverlys of this world, intercede.

Let's pray this prayer together:

> *Father, I bring Bob* [insert the name of the person you're praying for] *before You today. I am meeting with You to ask You to meet with him. He needs to be reconciled to You. You met with people in the Bible, and they were never the same. Please do that for Bob.*
> *I ask You to release the power of the Holy Spirit to break through every barrier, to heal every hurt, to open his eyes to truth, and to reconcile him to Yourself.*
> *As one of Your ambassadors on Earth, I ask this in the name of Christ, who has already paid the price for Bob's salvation.*
> *Amen.*

Did You Understand?

1. Can you explain the connection between boundaries, horizons, destinies and intercession?

2. What is the purpose of intercession?

3. How does the fall of humankind through Adam relate to intercessory prayer?

4. How does intercessory prayer further the spreading of the gospel?

5. Have you been to any prayer "meetings" lately?

Chapter Five

The Prize of Intercession

*By prayer, the bitterest enemies of the gospel have become
its most valiant defenders, the most wicked the truest sons of
God, and the most contemptible women the purest saints.
Oh, the power of prayer to reach down, where hope itself
seems vain, and lift men and women up into fellowship with and
likeness to God! It is simply wonderful! How little
we appreciate this marvelous weapon!*[1]

A young mother's efforts to raise her son righteously had
seemed to fail. All her pleadings to him concerning his de-
viant lifestyle seemingly fell on deaf ears. Yet her prayers
prevailed, and this immoral youth became the great man
of God, St. Augustine.

Along with others, the evangelist John Livingston
spent the whole night of June 21, 1630, in prayer. When
he preached the next day, 500 people were converted
to Christ.

The night before Jonathan Edwards preached his famous "Sinners in the Hands of an Angry God" message,
many members of his church devoted the entire night to
prayer. The Holy Spirit moved so powerfully during that
sermon, revealing the holiness and sovereignty of God, that
the elders desperately clung to the pillars of the church and
cried, "Lord, save us, we are slipping down to hell!"[2]

The greatest prize of our intercession is people meeting Christ as their Lord and Savior! In the previous chapter, we saw that intercession creates meetings between God and humans. The most important meeting that can possibly occur is when God meets with an unsaved person for the purpose of his or her conversion or salvation.

I agree with Dick Eastman, one of my heroes of the faith: All of us who know Christ as Savior are products of intercession. As he states in his book *Love on Its Knees*, we are first of all born-again followers of Jesus because He was our "go-between"—or intercessor—when He sacrificed His life on the cross. We are also born-again believers because of the powerful impact other intercessors have had on our lives throughout the years, whether or not we have been aware of it, defeating Satan's strategies and bringing us to a full knowledge of Christ.[3]

Eastman's personal testimony powerfully portrays how one's life can be drastically changed through the intercession of another person—in his case, his mother. At the age of 14, he had become involved in a life of rebellion and burglary. He and another young man had developed an effective scheme to prey upon unsuspecting patrons at the swimming pool, unobtrusively stealing purses or wallets while their owners were swimming.

One day, however, when his partner in crime called to set up their next time of stealing, Eastman suddenly realized he could no longer be involved in this kind of behavior. He couldn't explain why, but he knew he could never do anything like that again. Somehow, he knew his life was changing. His mother's intercession, standing against Satan's plans and praying for God to be truly revealed to her son, had prevailed. While the other young man was caught stealing and went to jail, Eastman went to church that evening as God began to answer his mother's prayers.[4]

Eastman is convinced that intercessory prayer is involved in *every* soul ever brought to a knowledge of Christ. Of course it is! God works on the earth through prayer, and you are going to have the awesome privilege of partnering with God to see people meet Christ. People will be in heaven because of your prayers. This is part of your destiny as a Christian. The enemy of prayer, Satan, will try to convince you that your prayers aren't accomplishing anything, but he is a liar.

In Acts 10, an angel visited a man named Cornelius and said, "Your prayers . . . have ascended as a memorial before God . . . your prayer has been heard" (vv. 4,31). This man's prayers resulted in salvation taking place for the first time in the Gentile (non-Jewish) world. The Holy Spirit fell upon them (see v. 44), causing a glorious meeting between God and people, all because God heard one man's prayers.

He is going to hear your prayers, as well, and God meetings will result! Paul told Timothy in 1 Timothy 2:4 that "God desires all men to be saved and to come to the knowledge of the truth." He had just told Timothy to pray for "all men" (v. 1). The connection is obvious: Prayer is the key to salvation. Let's look at six things we must ask for as we intercede for the lost.

First, we must pray that their spiritual eyes will be opened to truly see and understand the gospel. The apostle Paul said a part of his mission to the lost was "to open their eyes so that they may turn from darkness to light and from the dominion of Satan to God" (Acts 26:18). Again, in 2 Corinthians 4:4, the Holy Spirit said, "In whose case the god of this world has blinded the minds of the unbelieving, that they might not see the light of the gospel of the glory of Christ, who is the image of God."

We are told that there is a veil or covering over the minds of unbelievers, keeping them from understanding God (see 2 Cor. 4:3). Another verse, 1 Corinthians 2:14, states emphatically that they "*cannot* understand" (emphasis added) the spiritual realm—and therefore the things concerning God—apart from a supernatural revelation.

Interestingly, the biblical words "veil" and "revelation" come from the same Greek word.[5] A revelation is a "*lifting of the veil*" or an *uncovering*. In other words, that which was formerly covered has now been revealed.

We must pray that the eyes of unsaved people will be opened (revelation) in order that they may see Christ and His gospel clearly. This must be more than an intellectual grasping, but rather an understanding that penetrates the heart. Only then will a person have true biblical faith that is of the heart, not just the mind. Romans 10:8-10 describes this revelation and the transforming faith it produces:

> But what does it say? "The word is near you, in your mouth and in your *heart*"—that is, the word of faith which we are preaching, that if you confess with your mouth Jesus as Lord, and believe in your *heart* that God raised Him from the dead, you shall be saved; for with the *heart* man believes, resulting

in righteousness, and with the mouth he confesses, resulting in salvation" (emphasis added).

Closely associated with the first prayer need, *the second thing we must ask for is that all deception be broken off unbelievers*. Second Corinthians 10:4-5 tells us our spiritual weapons are "divinely powerful for . . . destroying speculations" in those under Satan's dominion. The phrase "destroying speculations" is not one easily understood without further definition.

Throughout this book, I have simply footnoted most of the Greek and Hebrew words, so as not to weigh you down with technical details. However, in this case, I need to include the actual Greek in order to point out its relationship to other references.

The Greek word for "speculation"—*logismos*—means any logic, philosophy or belief system imbedded deeply into the mind of a person. Our English word "logic" actually comes from this Greek word. The concept in this word goes beyond *what* a person thinks, to embody *why* he thinks it, as well. More than what he believes, it is why he believes it; it is not just how he acts, but why he acts that way.

These mindsets can be caused by what has been repeatedly taught, such as doctrines, religions, atheism, or any number of other beliefs. They can also be caused by what a person experiences: sexual fantasies and perversions, rejection, witchcraft, prejudices, and others. Any experience or observed pattern of behavior can so powerfully embed itself into the mind and emotions that it creates a pattern of thinking. People often don't even realize they have these paradigms or belief systems.

These *logismoses* can so control a person's thinking that any hearing of the gospel is first filtered through them, causing the message heard to actually be distorted. In other words, people don't hear only what we preach; they hear what we communicate plus what they already believe. For example, when a Jewish person is told that Jesus is the Messiah, at the same time that person hears this, he or she also remembers years of adamant teaching that He is not the Messiah. That *logismos*—philosophy, belief system—keeps Jews from believing in Christ. We must pray against these deceptions, asking God to destroy them and believing that the weapons unleashed through prayer are "divinely powerful for the destruction of fortresses" (2 Cor. 10:4).

The apostle Paul uses a different form of *logismos* in three separate but similar prayer requests. A look at them will make even clearer this need in unbelievers:

- Pray on my behalf, that utterance [*logos*] may be given to me in the opening of my mouth, to make known with boldness the mystery of the gospel (Eph. 6:19).

- Devote yourselves to prayer, keeping alert in it with an attitude of thanksgiving; praying at the same time for us as well, that God may open up to us a door for the Word [*logos*], so that we may speak forth the mystery of Christ, for which I have also been imprisoned; *in order that I may make it clear in the way I ought to speak* (Col. 4:2-4, emphasis added).

· Finally, brethren, pray for us that the Word [*logos*] of the Lord may spread rapidly and be glorified, just as it did also with you (2 Thess. 3:1).

It is easy to see the similarity of *logismos* and *logos*. They do indeed come from the same word. Paul is saying, in essence, "Pray that I am able to share the *logic* of the gospel in such a clear and powerful way that it overcomes the unbelievers' personal *logic* or belief system."

We are instructed to pray two ways where this matter is concerned:

1. Pray that the belief systems, philosophies or logic of unbelievers that contradict God's Word will be overcome.

2. Pray that the logic of God's Word will become clear and irresistible when shared with them.

We can see from these verses and conclusions that our intercession affects both the hearer of the message and the ability of the person sharing the gospel. Intercession is important for both aspects of the process. Great soul-winners of the past understood this and relied not only on preaching, but also looked to the power of prayer, as did the apostle Paul.

Charles Finney, who saw hundreds of thousands of people saved in his meetings, had a partner named Daniel Nash, generally known as Father Nash. Nash often accompanied Finney to his meetings, not to administrate or preach, but to pray. At times he went ahead of Finney, spending several days in prayer before the meetings began. In the book *Revival Lectures*, Finney talks about Nash:

> Having experienced a terrible overhaul of his own spiritual experience, Nash emerged from a cold and backslidden condition to faithfully labor for souls, full of the power of prayer. He prayed daily— often many times a day—for those whom he was led to place on his list, frequently literally in agony for them. Multitudes were thus converted, many of them hardened, abandoned characters who could not be reached in any ordinary way. One such example involved a bartender violently opposed to revival meetings who would deliberately swear outrageously whenever Christians were within hearing. It was so bad that some of his neighbors considered moving because they could not tolerate such swearing. When Father Nash heard of this situation, he became very grieved and took this man on in prayer. Day and night he labored in prayer for this ungodly bartender. Several days later, the tavern keeper came to a meeting, confessed his sins, and came to Christ. His confession was one of the most heartbroken they had ever heard, and seemed to cover the whole ground of his treatment of God, Christians, revival, and everything good. His barroom immediately became the place where prayer meetings were held.[6]

The third thing we must ask for when interceding for the lost is that *the stronghold of pride in them will be torn down.*

Second Corinthians 4:4 states, "The god of this world has blinded the minds of the unbelieving." Interestingly, the Greek word translated "blinded" has in its meaning the concept of self-conceit or pride.

I can only assume this came to be because pride blinds us to our true conditions. I am certain it is a part of the sinful nature passed on to humans from Lucifer at the Fall. His sin, of course, was pride, which led to rebellion (see Isa. 14:12-15). This same motive—pride, or the exalting of self—came to humans at the Fall.

I am also certain that it is one of the primary hindrances that keep people from accepting Christ. Pride takes many forms: wanting to rule one's own life and therefore not wanting another Lord; refusing to acknowledge one's sinful condition and therefore one's need for a savior; and not wanting to turn from certain sinful pleasures or lifestyles.

The good news is that we have the authority to tear down this stronghold through intercession. Second Corinthians 10:4-5 tells us our spiritual weapons are "divinely powerful for the destruction of . . . every *lofty thing* raised up against the kingdom of God" (italics added). A "lofty thing"[7] is something exalted to a place of preeminence, and has the same root word as "Most High God." Used in this context, it is the condition in the human race that causes us to want to be our own "most high." Quite simply, it is pride.

The Holy Spirit is saying that we, through our spiritual weapons of prayer, can demolish this stronghold in unbelievers. A sample prayer might be as follows: "In Jesus' name, I war against the stronghold of pride in Joe that blinds him to the light of the gospel. Holy Spirit, I ask You with Your great power to demolish the pride in him that exalts itself against the kingdom of God. I ask it based on your Word in 2 Corinthians 10:4-5."

The following story as relayed by Kenneth Hagin gives evidence of the effectiveness of praying this way for unbelievers:

> I saw what I had to do for my brother, Dub. I'd been fasting and praying that God would save him off and on for fifteen years, and if it ever did any good, I couldn't tell it. Anything you could mention, he'd done. I knew if it would work on him, it would work on anyone.
>
> I rose up off the bed with my Bible in one hand, and the other hand lifted, saying, "In the Name of the Lord Jesus Christ, I break the power of the devil over my brother Dub's life, and I claim his deliverance. [That means I claimed his deliverance from that blindness, that bondage of Satan.] And I claim his full salvation in the Name of the Lord Jesus Christ."
>
> Within three weeks, my brother was born again.
>
> Here is where intercession comes in—we are to loose the sinner from the blindness that he may see the light.
>
> If we can get people to see God as He really is, they'll want to love Him.
>
> We are one with the great Intercessor in His ministry of reconciliation.[8]

The fourth thing we must pray for on behalf of the unsaved is that *all Satan's strategies and schemes will fail.*

Second Corinthians 10:5, the verse we have previously referred to, says, "we are taking every thought captive to the obedience of Christ." Again, the context of the passage refers to doing this for others through prayer, not just controlling our own thoughts.

The phrase is more easily understood when the broad meaning of the word "thought"[9] is realized. Along with thought, it also means a plan, plot, scheme or device. The verse is telling us to war in prayer against every thought, scheme or plan of Satan's that would keep a person from submitting to Christ. In short, we pray that all of his strategies and schemes will fail. The following story relates how Nell's parents successfully warred in prayer against Satan's schemes for their daughter:

Although Nell had a Christian upbringing, her fascination with holistic health and diets led her into a New Age cult. Declaring that they would battle Satan with everything in them until the god of this world stopped blinding their daughter, Nell's parents daily interceded for her. They asked God to bring to her remembrance all the truth she'd learned as a young girl, and praised Him for being a covenant-keeping God.

One day Nell wandered into a Christian bookstore to buy some cookbooks, and the owner convinced her to purchase a little book. Later, she noticed it contained Scripture verses that the author suggested reading three times a day, like you would take vitamins. Being into anything that promoted health, Nell did this. Before long those

Scripture verses became more important to her than anything else.

Five months from the time her parents began intercession for Nell, she decided to start life over again with Jesus. She's since graduated from Bible school and has ministered in several countries.

"How easy it was to get deceived when I stopped going to church, praying every day, and reading my Bible," she admits. "But thank God, my eyes were opened to the truth."[10]

Fifth, we must also pray that the *Holy Spirit will hover around or envelop the unsaved person with His power and love.* This will break evil strongholds, release revelation, and draw this person to Christ. The words "hover" and "envelop" are carefully chosen to convey an important truth. Without overloading you with too much technical information, a compilation summary of several verses will give tremendous insight to this.

The Holy Spirit is the birthing agent of the triune God. When we are born again, the Scriptures describe it as being "born of the Spirit" (John 3:3-8). It was the Holy Spirit who "hovered" or "brooded"[11] over the earth at Creation, bringing forth all that was created. Elsewhere this act is referred to as a travail or a birthing. Amazingly enough, our prayers of intercession release the Holy Spirit (He who brings about the new birth or new creation) to brood or hover over unbelievers and release all that is necessary for them to be born again (see John 3:5-8; Gen. 1:2; Ps. 90:2; Isa. 66:7-9).

Paul prayed for the Galatians, causing their birth into God's family. That is why he called them his children and said he was in labor or travail in order that Christ be formed in them (see Gal. 4:19). His birthing intercession at this point was for their spiritual maturity, the forming of Christ into their actions and beliefs.

Elijah was used in this way in 1 Kings 18:41-46. A three-year drought came to an end through his birthing intercession. His very posture of prayer was that of a travailing woman in his day giving birth (see v. 42). The symbolism is unmistakable. His prayers released the Holy Spirit to bring forth, or birth, rain.

How much more should we consistently and fervently ask the Holy Spirit to release His spiritual rain on unbelievers, pouring Himself on them (see Joel 2:23-29; Acts 2:16-21)! We must ask Him to hover around them, breaking the strongholds—all beliefs, the root of pride, demonic thoughts, and strategies—in their lives, releasing revelation (the unveiling) and causing them to believe in Christ. Believe me, you won't have to persuade Him; He is waiting anxiously to release the fruit of Calvary.

The birth of the Church—the pouring out of the Holy Spirit at Pentecost—was a direct result of Christ asking the Father to send Him (see John 14:16). What an incredible testimony of God's mandated order that He will work on the earth through prayer! Ask!

Finally, we must *ask for workers—harvesters—to be sent to unbelievers.*

> And seeing the multitudes, He felt compassion for them, because they were distressed and downcast like sheep without a shepherd. Then He said to His disciples, "The harvest is plentiful, but the

workers are few. Therefore beseech the Lord of the harvest to send out workers into His harvest" (Matt. 9:36-38).

Because of God's decision to work on Earth through humanity's prayers and actions, even laborers in the harvest cannot be taken for granted. We are told to ask for them. Ask the Holy Spirit to send workers to those for whom you are praying. He is faithful to do so, and many are waiting to hear.

The ministry of Wycliffe Bible Translators has sent many workers into the harvest fields of the earth. These linguists live among illiterate tribes in order to master their native languages, reduce these languages to writing, and then translate the Word of God into the native tongues of the people. The following story occurred in New Guinea, where Marilyn and Judy were learning the Sepik Iwam language.

The tribespeople were fascinated by the girls' note-taking as they pointed to objects, asked their names, and then wrote them down phonetically. The pencil they were using was called a *thorn*; the paper they wrote on was a *banana leaf*; the act of writing itself was *carving*.

It took six months to impart to the tribe what the girls were really after. One day an elderly man could restrain his curiosity no longer. Shyly, he came up to say, "Mama Marilyn, what are you carving on that banana leaf with that thorn?" Patiently, Marilyn replied, "With this thorn we are carving your talk on this banana leaf so we can learn your talk and teach your people to carve it. Later we will give you God's talk on this banana leaf, just as He speaks it—and in your language."

Incredulous, the old man gently touched the paper and said, "You mean that God's talk and our talk can be carved on the banana leaf for us to see and understand?" Assured that this was so, he turned away, hesitated a moment to shake his head, then said softly, "Why did it take you so long to come?"[12]

I know one reason. Our prayers are a critical factor in getting laborers into the harvest. Millions of people are still waiting to hear the Good News of Jesus Christ. Be a part of the birthing of this, both for those you know and for the millions you don't know.

The prize awaits!

Let's pray this prayer together:

Father, I meet with You today on behalf of Bob [insert the name of the person for whom you're praying]. *I know You want to save him. I am ready to do my part to see this happen. I ask You to lift the veil from his eyes, that he might see Christ clearly. Please break all deception caused by the false beliefs Satan and circumstances have created.* [If you know what they are, mention them.] *Please demolish the stronghold of pride in him. Help him to see how much You love him and how much he needs You. I ask You to thwart every scheme of Satan and every thought he plants in Bob's mind to deceive him. Send the Holy*

Spirit to hover all around him, releasing love and
power. Send others to Bob, as well,
to share Your love and words with him.
I thank You for doing this. I will continue to pray until
I see the breakthrough. I ask based on the finished
work of Christ, Bob's Savior.
Amen.

Did You Understand?

1. What is the word "veil" referring to in unbelievers?

2. How do the mindsets or belief systems of the
   unsaved work against them? How does pride
   work against them?

3. Can you make the connection between the
   hovering of the Holy Spirit at Creation and
   intercession for lost people?

4. What "prize" are you asking God for?

Chapter Six

The Place of Intercession

Ken Gaub was walking down the street when he heard a pay phone ringing. Curious, he stopped to answer it. To his astonishment, the operator stated, "Long distance call for Ken Gaub. Is he there?" After debating the impossibility of this situation, he finally took the call.

The caller, about to commit suicide, had prayed for help and thought of Ken's ministry. Not knowing how to contact him, she continued to write her suicide note. When numbers came to her mind, she wrote them down. Wondering if God was miraculously giving her Ken's phone number, she dialed them.

Amazed at reaching him, she asked, "Are you in your office in California?"

"My office is in Washington," replied Ken.

"Oh, well, where are you then?" she queried.

"Don't you know? You called me," he responded.

"I don't know what area I'm calling. I just dialed the number on this paper."

"Ma'am, I'm in a phone booth in Dayton, Ohio!"

Recognizing this encounter could have been arranged only by God, Ken began to counsel her. The Holy Spirit's presence flooded the phone booth, giving him wisdom beyond his ability, and she soon prayed the sinner's prayer, committing to live for the Lord.[1]

This is one of the most remarkable stories I've ever read about God's sovereign ability to lead us, even when we're unaware that it's happening. He can have us at the right place at the right time, orchestrating events in a most heavenly—or unearthly—way.

This also happened in the life of Jacob. The Genesis record of this event uses the Hebrew word *paga*, which reveals precious truths to us about what I call *the place of intercession*.

Another meaning of the Hebrew word for "intercession"—*paga*—is "to land or light upon." *Paga* can also include the concept of landing or coming upon *by chance*. Thus it can mean, "to chance or happen upon." It is used this way in Jacob's encounter with God in Genesis 28:10-19 (emphasis added):

Then Jacob departed from Beersheba and went toward Haran. And he *came to* [*KJV*, "lighted upon"] a certain place and spent the night there, because the sun had set; and he took one of the stones of the place and put it under his head, and lay down in that place. And he had a dream, and behold, a ladder was set on the earth with its top reaching to heaven; and behold, the angels of God were ascending and descending on it. And behold, the Lord stood above it and said, "I am the Lord, the God of your father Abraham and the God of Isaac; the land on which you lie, I will give it to you and to your descendants. Your descendants shall also be like the dust of the earth, and you shall spread out to the west and to the east and to the north and to the south; and in you and in your descendants shall all the families of the earth be blessed. And behold, I am with you, and will keep you wherever you go, and will bring you back to this land; for I will not leave you until I have done what I have promised you." Then Jacob awoke from his sleep and said, "Surely the Lord is in this place, and I did not know it." And he was afraid and said, "How awesome is this place! This is none other than the house of God, and this is the gate of heaven." So Jacob rose early in the morning, and took the stone that he had put under his head and set it up as a pillar, and poured oil on its top. And he called the name of that place Bethel; however, previously the name of the city had been Luz.

This is a wonderful passage of Scripture and one of the first times *paga* is used in the Bible. At least six enlightening features of the place of intercession can be seen in this fascinating story where Jacob *met* with God, when he *lighted upon* Bethel. Technically speaking, Jacob wasn't in prayer when this incident happened. However, the fact that *paga* is used to describe Jacob's happening upon this place where he had such a powerful meeting with God makes it a wonderfully symbolic picture of what happens at the place of intercession.

First, notice that *the place of intercession—the paga place—becomes the God place*. Places of prayer become houses of God, or places where He dwells. Jacob declared in amazement, "The Lord is in this place . . . this is none other than the house of God . . . and he called the name of that place Bethel" (Gen. 28:16-17,19). The name Bethel actually means the "house of God." In intercession (*paga*), a place is built for the presence of God to dwell. And as Jacob said, God's dwelling places are "awesome" (v. 17).

I have a friend who pastors in Walla Walla, Washington. He was preaching a powerful message in one of his services when a young new Christian became so overwhelmed with the revelation that he could no longer contain himself. Leaping to his feet, he began to loudly exclaim, "Awesome, dude! Awesome!"

I've had a few "Amens!" and a "Hallelujah!" or two in my messages, but I've yet to receive an "Awesome, dude!" I'm working on it, though.

Jacob said, "How awesome is this place!" When God shows up, whether at a phone booth or at a rock to announce a man's destiny, it is awesome. And God always shows up at the place of prayer. Many of my most life-changing encounters with God have been during times of intercession.

I recall a time years ago when I was with a friend who had done a lot of LSD. He began to have a terrible flashback—a recurring effect of this dangerous drug, causing strange and sometimes terrifying hallucinations. As he writhed uncontrollably, screaming and groaning in terror, great faith and righteous indignation rose up in me, and I began to intercede. After a few moments, he stopped suddenly, and a great peace came over him. He looked at me and described the hideous images he had been having, and the sudden change that came as I prayed.

God then immediately began to minister to *me*. His presence became awesome as He spoke to me about my future ministry. This was many years ago, and the things He revealed to me that day have come to pass. The encounter took place not in a church service or a devotional time, but in a short session of intercession.

When we move into the unselfish ministry of interceding for someone, God finds it irresistible and meets (*paga*) with us. He always loves our company, but when we begin to represent His beloved Son, the heart of the Father is stirred beyond His ability to resist. He simply must respond. Thus the ordinary place becomes an awesome place: the house of God.

Many things can be said about the presence of God. In it there is fullness of joy (see Ps. 16:11), safety (see Ps. 91:1-2), light (see 1 Tim. 6:16), and pleasures forevermore (see Ps. 16:11). Actually, all that can be said about God can be said about His presence, and intercession takes us there.

The second thing Jacob's story illustrates about the place of intercession is *God's willingness to bring precision or accuracy to our prayers*. Jacob "happened" upon Bethel, much like Ken Gaub happened upon the phone booth. He wasn't guided there by understanding or reasoning; he simply "chanced upon" (*paga*) it at sunset and, needing a place to sleep, spent the night there. He was, however, without being aware of it, being led by the Holy Spirit. Bethel was an important place in Israel and one where God intended Jacob's future to be shaped. He was brought there by the sovereign direction of the Holy Spirit. A more literal rendering of verse 11 actually would be "he came to *the* place," not just *a* place.

Remembering that this word for "coming upon by chance," *paga*, is also the word for "intercession," what does this say to us about prayer? We often do not have enough wisdom, understanding or insight to know exactly how to pray. Like Jacob, it's almost as if we must "chance upon" the right prayer. In these incidents, we can be assured that the Holy Spirit will help us and cause us to hit the mark.

I was astonished a few years ago while teaching an Old Testament course at Christ for the Nations Institute in Dallas, Texas, when an Israeli student raised his hand in class and gave me the following information. I had mentioned *paga*—intercession—and the fact that the Holy Spirit helps us hit the mark in our prayers. Using Hebrew words can be somewhat intimidating when doing so before someone who happens to speak it as his first language. My initial thought was that Avi might correct me. I was pleasantly relieved when instead he informed me that in target practicing in Israel, the word for "bull's-eye" is *paga*! Imagine that! The very word for "intercession" actually means "bull's-eye."

God will do for us what He did for Jacob. When we "don't know how to pray as we should" (Rom. 8:26), He will help us find the mark—the place—just as He helped Jacob. I recall the story of Steve (not his real name) who was very ill with many different problems: stomach pains, headaches, back pain, and other symptoms. Doctors could not solve the problems, and much prayer had been offered for Steve's healing, also with no results.

One day the Holy Spirit quietly spoke to an intercessor who was praying for him: "The problem isn't physical, it is spiritual. Steve has unforgiveness and bitterness toward a person who wronged him. Challenge him to forgive and release that person."

Steve was finally able to forgive the person who had hurt him. The results were amazing! A process of healing began that didn't stop until he was completely well.

Paga . . . bull's-eye . . . Holy Spirit accuracy. The intercessor had "chanced" upon the problem. What she couldn't know, the Holy Spirit knew, and He caused her to "land upon" (*paga*) the right place. That is effective Spirit-led intercession.

Jesus told us to end our prayers with "For Thine is the kingdom, power, and glory forever." The word "power" in this phrase also means "ability." He was reminding us that we don't have the ability to accomplish what is needed in our own strength and understanding. Only the Father does. We must lean on Him for our ability to hit the mark.

Another great truth found in Jacob's encounter is that *through intercession, heaven and Earth are connected.* In his dream, Jacob saw a ladder extending from Earth up to heaven, with angels ascending and descending on it. The activity of heaven was being released to Earth. Jesus said to pray for this when He taught us to ask for God's kingdom to come and His will to be done on Earth as it is in heaven (see Matt. 6:10).

Jacob said this place was "the gate of heaven" (Gen. 28:17). He realized it was an entry point for God's will to penetrate Earth. *Paga places become gates to heaven where God's will is released onto the earth.*

We dealt with this somewhat in the previous chapter—the connecting or meeting of heaven and Earth through intercession—so we need not say much about it here. Suffice it to say that intercession joins heaven and Earth, releasing the will of God into situations.

This leads us, however, into the next great truth in this story. *In the place of intercession, divine-human partnerships are formed.* Not only were heaven and Earth connected, but God also told Jacob that He was going to greatly bless him: "and in you and in your descendants shall all the families of the earth be blessed" (Gen. 28:14). A part of our destiny as Christians is the privilege of partnering with God in helping others find their destinies. God wants to bless others through our efforts and prayers.

When George McCluskey married and started a family, he decided to invest one hour a day in prayer, because he wanted his kids to follow Christ. After a time, he expanded his prayers to include his grandchildren and great-grandchildren. Every day between 11:00 a.m. and noon, he prayed for the next three generations.

As the years went by, his two daughters committed their lives to Christ and married men who went into full-time ministry. The two couples produced four girls and one boy. Each of the girls married a minister, and the boy became a pastor.

The first two children born to this generation were both boys. Upon graduation from high school, the two cousins chose the same college and became roommates. During their sophomore year, one boy decided to go into the ministry. The other didn't. He undoubtedly felt some pressure to continue the family legacy, but he chose instead to pursue his interest in psychology.

He earned his doctorate and eventually wrote books for parents that became bestsellers. He started a radio program heard on more than a thousand stations each day. The man's name—James Dobson.[2]

Witness the power of prayer! George McCluskey partnered with God in the place of intercession, and God's destiny for James Dobson was realized. His ministry has indeed blessed many families of the earth. The next time you're blessed by Focus on the Family or by one of Dr. Dobson's books, thank God for the intercession of George McCluskey.

Another important truth about *paga* places is that *angelic activity is released* there. "And behold, a ladder was set on the earth with its top reaching to heaven; and behold, the angels of God were ascending and descending on it" (Gen. 28:12). Thetus Tenney, in her book *Prayer Takes Wings*, relates a story about two men who were protected from harm through the intervention of angels:

Dave Wright and Eddy Wiese had attended a church service in Oklahoma and were flying home to Fort Worth, Texas, in a Beechcraft Bonanza plane. Alerted to the possibility of threatening weather, the believers in Oklahoma were covering them in prayer. As the men prepared to land, a strong downdraft caused the plane to collide with a power line and crash. The men ran to safety—amazingly, the only injury to them was a minor cut. When they looked back, expecting to see the plane explode, they saw two extremely large men dressed in grayish white robes, hovering over the plane. These angels had undoubtedly delivered the men from destruction, as a result of the intercession of others.[3]

The building of altars for our lives is another truth seen in this story about the place of intercession. "So Jacob rose early in the morning, and took the stone that he had put under his head and set it up as a pillar, and poured oil on its top" (Gen. 28:18). The word "pillar" could be translated as a memorial stone or a monument. In Old Testament times, altars were built not only as places of sacrifice but also as memorials to mark and remember significant events. We do much the same today in building memorials at great battle sites or in memory of great leaders.

Joshua erected two memorials where he and Israel crossed the Jordan River into Canaan (see Josh. 4:8-9). Abraham built an altar to the Lord at Shechem where God first promised him the land of Canaan: "And the Lord appeared to Abram and said, 'To your descendants I will give this land.' So he built an altar there to the Lord who had appeared to him" (Gen. 12:7).

The prophet Samuel built a memorial near the town of Mizpah to mark a victory the Lord gave Israel over the Philistines (see 1 Sam. 7:12). He named it Ebenezer, meaning, "the stone of help," stating, "thus far the Lord has helped us."

How does this altar-building relate to us today? Are we supposed to build literal altars or memorials? That, of course, isn't necessary. Yet we do build them in our hearts.

In my first book, *Intercessory Prayer*, I tell the story of a young girl who had been in a comatose state for two-and-a-half years. Her brain was basically destroyed, eaten up by infection caused by viral encephalitis. After a year of intense and persistent intercession, to the amazement of the medical world, the Lord restored her to complete health. After spending 60 to 70 hours praying over her during a one-year period, I will never forget the day I saw her awake and alert. . . . I built a memorial there.

Today, when nagging doubts try to trouble my mind to convince me that God will not come through for me in a particular situation, I revisit my Ebenezer. Quietly I whisper, "Thus far He has helped me."

I have many such altars. One stands in Guatemala where the little girl (mentioned in chapter 2) used to be tied to the tree. Another stands at the place where I prayed for my wife, Ceci, and God healed her of an ovarian cyst. I also "built" one where I first met her, and where each of our daughters, Sarah and Hannah, was born. There are many others, all standing as monuments to the faithfulness of God in my life.

You'll build your own. As you live a life of intercession, creating meetings between your God and other individuals, lighting on Bethels where destinies are shaped as heaven meets Earth, or simply receiving personal help from your faithful Father, you'll find many appropriate places to erect Ebenezers. Build them strong enough to stand the test of time and tall enough to be seen from far away.

Let's pray this prayer together:

Father, I know I'm Your partner and that my
prayers join heaven and Earth. At times I feel so
inadequate when praying for [insert your situation],
but I know You want to help me. Enter my prayer
time; make this place a Bethel. Cause my prayers to
hit the mark. Give me Your thoughts and wisdom
as I pray. I ask for angelic help in this situation.
[Now, wait upon the Lord and then begin to pray
as He directs you. Be bold and ask in faith—
He will do as you have asked.]
Amen.

Did You Understand?

1. What connects the story of Jacob in Genesis 28 with intercession?

2. What is a gate of heaven? What does this have to do with intercession?

3. How does a bull's-eye relate to prayer?

4. Have you built any memorial altars lately?

Chapter Seven

The Protection of Intercession

We visited Disney World this past summer. Along with the excitement of heat, humidity, long lines and high prices, I had the adventure of visiting the Tower of Terror. This ride simulates an earthquake as experienced while riding in a hotel elevator. It was everything but uplifting.

A few years ago I visited the Tower of London in England. A fortress on the River Thames, this bastion has served in historic times as everything from a palace to a prison. We saw the crown jewels and, as a reminder to those who might try to steal them, many ancient instruments of execution and torture. I've never moved from exhilaration to excruciation so quickly. I mumbled, "God save the Queen," and hastily departed.

I've also visited the Eiffel Tower in Paris, a 984-foot-high tower of iron framework, built for the International Exposition of 1889. Demonstrating my linguistic skills and cultural awareness, while gazing at this incredible accomplishment, I shouted to those with me, "Vive la France, birthplace of the French fry."

The following story offers an interesting assessment of an infamous tower in the Bible—Babel:

An eminent architect was under cross-examination at a trial concerning a building he had designed. One of the prosecutors, attempting to distract the man during his testimony, asked, "Are you a builder?"

Immediately the witness replied, "No, sir, I am an architect."

"But they are much the same, aren't they?" the prosecutor added.

"I beg your pardon, sir, but in my opinion they are totally different."

"Oh, indeed! Perhaps you will explain the difference?"

To this the witness responded, "An architect, sir, conceives the design, prepares the plan, draws all to specifications, and in short, supplies the mind. The builder is merely the bricklayer or the carpenter. The builder is the machine; the architect, the power that puts it together and sets it going."

"Oh, very well, Mr. Architect, that will do. And now, after your very ingenious distinction between the two, perhaps you can inform the court, who was the architect of the Tower of Babel?"

The witness promptly responded, "There was no architect, sir, only builders. That's why there was so much confusion."[1]

This is not totally accurate, of course, but it is an interesting and humorous observation.

Another tower in the Scriptures is known not for its terror, jewels, pride or confusion, but as a place of strength and safety: "The name of the Lord is a strong tower; the righteous runs into it and is safe" (Prov. 18:10). Psalm 61:3 calls our God "a tower of strength against the enemy."

This chapter is about the protection available to us through intercession. One of the meanings of the Hebrew word for "intercession," *paga*, is "boundary" or "border." Consistent with the definition "to meet," it is the point at which two territories meet or connect. Hence, a boundary, or, as *The Spirit-Filled Bible* says, the extent to which a boundary reaches. *Paga* is used repeatedly this way in Joshua 19.

In the context of intercessory prayer, *paga* is the establishing of boundaries or walls of protection and the marking of a territory as one's own, declaring, "I will not permit intruders or interlopers." I love Psalm 91:1-4 from *THE MESSAGE*:

> You who sit down in the High God's presence, spend the night in Shaddai's shadow, say this: "God, you're my refuge. I trust in you and I'm safe!" That's right—he rescues you from hidden traps, shields you from deadly hazards. His huge outstretched arms protect you—under them you're perfectly safe; his arms fend off all harm.

Wow, what a promise!

A missionary determined to take the gospel to an interior region of China experienced the sovereign protection of God. Ruthless bandits along the road had prevented this area from being reached. However, this young missionary went, preaching the Good News of Jesus Christ. He later returned to the base without having seen any bandits. Shortly thereafter, the missionaries heard a rumor circulating throughout the area: the bandits had not attacked because an entourage of eleven soldiers had traveled with him. As he had traveled alone, the missionaries concluded angels must have protected him; but why eleven?

The missionary wrote about this experience to his home church in the United States. His pastor asked when this had happened. Upon receiving this information, the pastor excitedly communicated his part of the story. The pastor had been prompted by God to call a special prayer meeting for this missionary. When the date of the prayer meeting arrived, the pastor was disappointed at the poor turnout. That changed after he received the missionary's amazing report. The pastor was thrilled to tell him, "You'll be pleased to know that, counting myself, there were exactly eleven of us who were praying for you that very day."[2]

Those 11 faithful intercessors became a wall, or perimeter of protection, around this missionary through their prayers of intercession. Through them, Psalm 91 and Proverbs 18:10 became reality. God wants us, also, to believe in the power of the name of Jesus and to use it to build walls of protection around individuals.

Isaiah 26:1 and 60:18 speak of God's protection as walls: "In that day this song will be sung in the land of Judah: 'We have a strong city; He sets up walls and ramparts for security.' " "Violence will not be heard again in your land, nor devastation or destruction within your borders; but you will call your walls salvation, and your gates praise."

In his book *Prayer That Moves Mountains*, Gordon Lindsay tells a remarkable story similar to the one about the missionary to China. It is a literal picture of building walls of protection through prayer:

> Unknown to a Christian Armenian, bandits followed his caravan as he transported merchandise across the desert to a town in Turkish Armenia. The bandits waited until after dark to attack, but upon approaching the caravan they were astonished to see high walls surrounding it. The same scenario happened on the following day, with high walls again protecting the caravan at night. On the third night, however, the walls were broken in places, allowing the bandits access to the merchant. Frightened by the mystery of the walls, the leader of the bandits offered to spare the merchant and his caravan if he would just share the secret of the walls with him. Having no knowledge of the walls, the merchant replied that all he knew was that each evening he prayed, committing himself and those with him to God, but that on this particular evening he had not prayed as usual, due to his tiredness, and that probably accounted for the breaks in the wall. This testimony so amazed the bandits that they gave their lives to Christ and became God-fearing men.[3]

Many would find this story unbelievable. Yet why should it surprise us? God simply allowed people to see what was truly there in the spirit realm: walls of protection. Zechariah 2:5 calls them walls of fire: " 'For I,' declares the Lord, 'will be a wall of fire around her, and I will be the glory in her midst.' "

Supernatural protections, as illustrated by these stories, occur as intercessors learn to become sensitive to the promptings of the Holy Spirit, which alert them to pray for others in critical times of need. This call from the Holy Spirit can come through a sense of foreboding or uneasiness concerning a certain individual, as well as simply by hearing the voice of the Holy Spirit telling us to pray for someone.

Set in the context of spiritual warfare, the Holy Spirit speaks of this in Ephesians 6:18: "With all prayer and petition pray at all times in the Spirit, and with this in view, be on the alert with all perseverance and petition for all the saints." The word "times" is the Greek word *kairos*, which means "strategic or opportune time." He is saying that, in light of the warfare we're in, we must be alert for Satan's attacks against others and must pray at all these *kairoses*, or strategically timed attacks. This is what happened with the missionary in China. The pastor was alert and sensed the need to pray for him. His 11 intercessors will, no doubt, share in the missionary's reward.

The implication of Ephesians 6:18 is clear: If we're alert, the Holy Spirit will warn us. If we pray, He'll intervene. Hebrews 4:16 tells us we'll find grace to help us in these strategic times of need.[4] The Hebrew counterpart to the Greek word *kairos* is *eth*, which is a Hebrew word for "strategic time." Used in Psalm 9:9, God tells us He is "a stronghold in the times of trouble."[5]

Oral Roberts experienced the Holy Spirit's intervention during a *kairos* attack against his family:

> After ministering at a conference over a thousand miles away from home, Oral had gone to bed in his hotel when he was suddenly awakened and heard these words, "Your wife and children in Tulsa are in serious danger. Pray." He spent time in deep intercession for his family until he finally felt the burden lift. When he returned home to Tulsa, his wife, Evelyn, told him that one night, after the children and she had gone to bed, she heard someone trying to break into their home. Paralyzed with fright, she had been unable to do anything other than to pray for God's help and for Oral to be alerted to pray for them. Thankfully, the intruder had left without ever entering the house. As they compared their experiences, the Robertses realized that Oral had been awakened and alerted to pray at the exact time that Evelyn had heard the intruder.[6]

Now that is a *kairos* attack and a *kairos* answer to a *paga* prayer! Walls or boundaries of protection were established through intercession, and God's promise of protection was fulfilled. Never assume that a warning such as this is just your imagination. Always pray.

In her book *Listen, God Is Speaking to You*, Quin Sherrer tells of a friend who heard the warning of the Lord for her home and prayed during the *kairos* time:

> I was rooming with Ruthie at a Christian confer-
> ence when she told me how God had protected
> her property. One night during the church serv-
> ice she heard a voice: *"Your house is being robbed."*
> She tried to dismiss the thought. She'd lived in
> that house for thirty years and there had been no
> burglaries in her neighborhood. But the more she
> thought about it, the more it seemed to her that
> the inner voice she had heard was the Holy Spirit
> warning her.
>
> "Lord, if our house is being robbed, please
> send an angel—no, Lord, send a warring angel—to
> frighten the burglar off." Then she began to quote
> Scriptures, praying for protection: "No evil will
> come near our dwelling place. . . . No weapon
> formed against us shall prosper . . ."
>
> Sure enough, when she and her husband ar-
> rived home, their back patio door was smashed in
> and everything inside was in disarray—drawers
> open and stuff scattered everywhere. The next
> day, when the police officer came to get a list of
> the things they knew were missing, all they had to
> report was one pillowcase. He told them that's
> what a burglar usually takes to stash the valu-
> ables. "As far as we can tell nothing is missing—
> not even my good gold jewelry," Ruthie told him.
>
> He looked around at her china, silver, and
> gold vases. "With all these beautiful things, I
> don't understand why you weren't robbed blind.

Something obviously frightened away the intruder.
He left in a hurry," the policeman said.

Two other houses in her neighborhood were
robbed that night. Ruthie is sure God sent a war-
ring angel of protection, as she had prayed and
asked Him to do.[7]

That is *paga*! Protective intercession and building
walls of protection through prayer. You, too, can be used
by the Lord in this way. The key is learning to listen to
the Holy Spirit. This story reminds me of Psalm 27:1-3
from *THE MESSAGE*:

Light, space, zest—that's God! So, with him on my
side I'm fearless, afraid of no one and nothing.
When vandal hordes ride down ready to eat me
alive, those bullies and toughs fall flat on their
faces. When besieged, I'm calm as a baby. When all
hell breaks loose, I'm collected and cool.

The apostle Paul was a firm believer in receiving protective and deliverance prayers from others, in strategic as
well as in general times of need. He frequently requested
prayer from those with whom he was in relationship. Romans 15:30-31 states:

Now I urge you, brethren, by our Lord Jesus Christ
and by the love of the Spirit, to strive together
with me in your prayers to God for me, *that I
may be delivered* from those who are disobedient

in Judea, and that my service for Jerusalem may prove acceptable to the saints (emphasis added).

Again in Philippians 1:19, Paul states his confidence of "deliverance through your prayers." Also, in Philemon 1:22 he says, "I hope that through your prayers I shall be given to you." Paul was frequently persecuted and imprisoned for his preaching of the gospel. He placed his hope of deliverance from some of this in the prayers of his friends. He believed in the power of intercession, not just for the furthering of the gospel but also for protection.

The apostle Peter was protected from certain death in Acts 12. Herod had arrested James, one of the 12 disciples of Christ, and had him killed. When he saw how much this pleased the Jews, he arrested Peter also, and planned to execute him as well. This prompted fervent prayer by the Church for Peter's release (see Acts 12:5).

The answer to their prayers for Peter's protection is one of the most amazing stories in the Bible. Angels visited Peter in his cell, caused his chains to fall off, somehow blinded the guards from seeing him, led him out of the jail, supernaturally opened the iron gate to the city, and departed from him. The entire ordeal was so supernatural, Peter at first thought it was only a vision.

Now that is *paga* extraordinaire!

Two ancient cities, both impregnable natural strongholds made of rock, exemplify the type of fortress the Lord wants to be to us. The city of Petra (Greek for "rock") "was virtually impregnable against attack by the military technology and weaponry of the ancient world," say Eastman and Hayford in their book *Living and Praying in Jesus' Name*.

The primary access to this stronghold was, and continues to be, a very narrow, natural gorge called the *Sik* (Arabic for "shaft") which is about a mile in length and approximately ten feet wide. Because of this geological factor, the Sik could easily be defended by even a tiny band of people against any invasion, even when the attackers used suicide tactics. As G.A. Smith notes in his commentary, "The interior is reached by defiles (gorges) so narrow that two horsemen may scarcely ride abreast, and the sun is shut out by the overhanging rocks."[8]

The original name of this city was Sela, the Hebrew word for "rock." The psalmist David used this analogy in Psalm 31:3. "Thou art my rock [*sela*]," he said. What an awesome picture of the Lord who is our hiding place of protection! He is our Petra, our city of refuge in times of trouble.

I have been to the second city, Masada (from the Hebrew word *metsudah*), which is an incredible natural fortress near the Dead Sea. King Herod used this as a military outpost, and in the first century A.D., it took a three-year siege for the Roman Empire to starve out a band of Jewish zealots from this amazing place.

Psalm 31:3, the same verse that states God is our Sela or Petra, also declares Him to be our Masada. "Thou art my *sela* [rock]," David said, "and my *metsudah* [fortress]." What an incredible picture of David's confidence in God as his strong protection!

David used another geographical illustration of God's protection in the famous twenty-third Psalm. He states in verse 4, "Even though I walk through the valley of the shadow of death, I fear no evil; for Thou art with me; Thy rod and Thy staff, they comfort me." *The International Standard Bible Encyclopedia* says the phrase "valley of the shadow of death" is the term used to describe the infamous valley to the southwest of Jerusalem where some of the people of Judah caused children to 'pass through the fire.' " Second Kings 23:10 mentions it as the valley where children were offered as sacrifices to the god Molech. *The International Standard Bible Encyclopedia* goes on to say, "Because of the atrocities that had been performed there, the name of this valley developed into a synonym for hell."[9]

This verse is also used, of course, to refer to security and comfort even in times of literal death. While valid, it should not be limited to this. David was stating his faith that when he walked through the most evil or difficult of places, he could trust God to be his protector.

The Lord Jesus wants to be a strong tower and an impregnable fortress for us as well. Intercession—*paga*—releases this protective force. Build the walls through prayer. Establish your perimeter. Pray daily for protection. Be alert to the promptings of the Holy Spirit and, when they come, pray.

A continuation of Psalm 91, mentioned earlier, is too powerful a promise not to include in this chapter:

His huge outstretched arms protect you—under them you're perfectly safe; his arms fend off all harm. Fear nothing— not wild wolves in the night, not flying arrows in the day; not disease that prowls through the darkness, not disaster that

erupts at high noon. Even though others suc-
cumb all around, drop like flies right and left, no
harm will even graze you. You'll stand untouched,
watch it all from a distance, watch the wicked
turn into corpses. Yes, because God's your refuge,
the High God your very own home, evil can't get
close to you, harm can't get through the door. He
ordered his angels to guard you wherever you go.
If you stumble, they'll catch you; their job is to
keep you from falling. You'll walk unharmed
among lions and snakes, and kick young lions
and serpents from the path. "If you'll hold on to
me for dear life," says God, "I'll get you out of
any trouble. I'll give you the best of care if you'll
only get to know and trust me. Call me and I'll
answer, be at your side in bad times; I'll rescue
you, then throw you a party. I'll give you a long
life, give you a long drink of salvation!" (Psalm
91:4-16, *THE MESSAGE*)

In his book *The Necessity of Prayer*, E. M. Bounds tells
the following story of a friend who was quite a lover of
the hunt:

"Rising early one morning," he said, "I heard the
barking of a number of dogs chasing deer. Looking at a large open field in front of me, I saw a
young fawn making its way across the field and
giving signs that its race was almost run. It leaped
over the rails of the enclosed place and crouched
within ten feet of where I stood. A moment later

two of the hounds came over, and the fawn ran in my direction and pushed its head between my legs. I lifted the little thing to my breast, and, swinging round and round, fought off the dogs. Just then I felt that all the dogs in the West could not and would not capture that fawn after its weakness had appealed to my strength." So is it when human helplessness appeals to Almighty God.[10]

Be like this helpless fawn. When the "hounds" of danger approach, run to the Lord as your powerful protector. Build your walls of protection through *paga*— intercession. Christ wants to be your strong tower.

Tower of Terror? London? Babel? Eiffel? Nah!

"Vive la paga!"

Let's pray this prayer together:

Father, thank You for the protection available through prayer. As I meet with You today, I ask You to make my home like an impenetrable city. In the name of Jesus, my strong tower, I place boundaries of protection around me and my family. [Use their names— be specific. Mention others who come to mind, or whom God has assigned to you for prayer.]

Father, are there any kairos situations You need me to pray about? I'm available to You at any time.

[Listen for any leading of the Holy Spirit.]

I love being Your friend and partner, God.

Thank You for the relationship we have.

In Christ's name I pray,

Amen.

Did You Understand?

1. Can you explain the connection between boundaries and intercessory prayer?

2. How does the concept of strategic time relate to prayer?

3. What do the ancient cities Masada and Petra exemplify?

4. Vive la *what?!*

Chapter Eight

The Power of Intercession

Hearing Jun Mon's cries of grief, the neighbors in this slum district outside Phnom Penh, Cambodia, knew that her husband, Khev Choen, had died. It came as no surprise, as his health had been steadily deteriorating, and he had been unconscious for the last few days. The witch doctor and herbal medicines—all the family could afford—had not been able to revive him, and now he was gone.

A couple of weeks earlier, a Christian house-church group had brought some hope. They had observed Jun Mon's despair as she sat outside her tumbledown one-room home, and, upon learning that her husband was about to die, Theavy Ser had led them in prayer for her. After hearing the gospel message, Jun Mon and her sister gladly accepted the Lord and were encouraged by the words of the Bible they received.

But now Khev Choen was dead. Late that night, while sitting with Jun Mon and her sister to comfort them, Theavy felt led to pray and to share Scripture passages with them about Christ's victory over death and the grave. After she left this young believer, Jun Mon continued to read about Jesus' miracles and then knelt by her husband's body. For three hours, Jun Mon and her sister wept and pleaded with God to restore life and health to him.

Although they had been praying for this miracle, they were shocked when Khev suddenly sat up in bed and declared that he was alive! And also healthy and hungry! After eating, he shared with them what he had experienced. Evidently at the same time that he stopped breathing, two men in black came and escorted him through darkness to a wide river. On the other side was a man with two books, one containing names of people who had died and the other holding names of people about to die. Khev was questioned, but then told to go back home. As he began his journey home, he realized his escorts were gone and that his spirit and steps lightened as he went. Suddenly he came to a fork in the road—darkness on one path and brilliant light on the other. In the background he could hear voices debating which way he would choose. He chose the path of light and, as he stepped onto it, he heard a door slam. The next thing he remembered was suddenly sitting up in his own bed.

When Theavy and others came later to help Jun Mon, they were ecstatic to see Khev alive and walking. Rejoicing at the resurrection power of God, they shared with Khev about Jesus Christ, and he committed himself to the One who had restored his life. Not surprisingly, the home church grew from 4 to 32 in just a few months. Khev, healthy and strong, is a walking testimony to the grace and power of God.[1]

A testimony to the grace and *power* of God? I'd say so!

As intercessors we need to understand the incredible power available to us. God has not asked us to represent Him on Earth without giving us the means to do it well. Amazing power can be released through intercession. A great verse in Job pictures this power in intercession: "He covers His hands with the lightning, and commands it to *strike the mark*" (Job 36:32, emphasis added).

The phrase "strike the mark" is translated from *paga*, our Hebrew word for "intercession." Awesome! When lightning flashes from God's presence, its striking the desired target is comparable to what happens in intercession.

Have you ever seen a tree struck by lightning? If so, you've seen a picture of intercession. I do lots of praying in a woods nearby. At times I come across trees struck by lightning. The lightning is so hot it literally changes the molecular structure of the trees and twists the trunks until they look like the stripes on a candy cane. The temperature in a lightning bolt can reach 30,000 degrees Celsius (45,000 degrees Fahrenheit), hotter than the surface of the sun. That's hot stuff! And God uses this to exemplify the *power of intercession!*

Habakkuk 3:4 also speaks of light flashing forth from the hand of God: "His radiance is like the sunlight: He has rays flashing from His hand, and there is the hiding of His power." The *Amplified* translation is also very descriptive: "And His brightness was like the sunlight; rays streamed from His hand, and there [in the sunlike splendor] was the hiding place of His power."[2]

I'm not trying to get weird with you, but our prayers really do release God's power in the form of spiritual lightning and cause both His judgments and His blessings to be brought forth.

The following Scriptures refer to this:

And when He had taken the book, the four living creatures and the twenty-four elders fell down before the Lamb, having each one a harp, and golden bowls full of incense, *which are the prayers of the saints* (Rev. 5:8, emphasis added).

And when He broke the seventh seal, there was silence in heaven for about half an hour. And I saw the seven angels who stand before God; and seven trumpets were given to them. And another angel came and stood at the altar, holding a golden censer; and much incense was given to him, that he might add it to *the prayers of all the saints* upon the golden altar which was before the throne. And the smoke of the incense, *with the prayers of the saints*, went up before God out of the angel's hand. And the angel took the censer; and he filled it with the fire of the altar and threw it to the earth; and there followed peals of thunder and sounds and slashes of *lightning* and an earthquake (Rev. 8:1-5, emphasis added).

Notice that our prayers release thunder, lightning and earthquakes. That qualifies as power! Dudley Hall comments on this phenomenon in his book *Incense and Thunder*:

Here's the picture of what prayer looks like in heaven. It looks like incense going up before the altar of God. Every time we lift our hearts toward God in Jesus' name, an angel of God takes the incense in his hand (our prayers), mixes it with fire from the altar of God, flings it back to the earth, and it enters the earth's atmosphere as spiritual thunder, lightning, and earthquakes. That should give us some encouragement to pray! God has chosen to partner with us in transferring heaven into earth.[3]

David also spoke of this in the psalms:

In my distress I called upon the Lord, and cried to my God for help; He heard my voice out of His temple, and my cry for help before Him came into His ears. Then the earth shook and quaked; and the foundations of the mountains were trembling and were shaken, because He was angry. Smoke went up out of His nostrils, and fire from His mouth devoured; coals were kindled by it. . . . And He rode upon a cherub and flew; and He sped upon the wings of the wind. . . . From the brightness before Him passed His thick clouds, hailstones and coals of fire. The Lord also thundered in the heavens, and the Most High uttered His voice, hailstones, and coals of fire. And He sent out His arrows, and scattered them, and lightning flashes in abundance, and routed them. . . . He delivered me from my strong enemy, and from those who hated me, for they were too mighty for me. They confronted me in the day of my calamity, but the Lord was my stay. He brought me forth also into a broad place; He rescued me, because He delighted in me (Ps. 18:6-8, 10,12-14,17-19).

Talk about power through prayer!

I don't know how David understood or saw these things. I'm sure they were happening in the spiritual realm, not the physical. God evidently allowed David to see into this realm so that he could record in Scripture this encouragement of what can happen when we pray.

Esther Ilnisky shares a wonderful story of God's power "striking the mark" to bring healing. (Please remember that "strike the mark" is a literal rendering of *paga*, the Hebrew word for "intercession.")

From a magnificent event in my childhood, I know God hears and *answers* the prayers of children.

Daisy was nine. I was four. But the memory is stark. All I knew was that my big sister couldn't move her arms or legs, and I was scared.

"Mr. and Mrs. Shabaz," the doctor's voice quivered, "your daughter is paralyzed. She will never walk again."

Undaunted, knowing instinctively what to do next, they gathered their son and four daughters together and called the pastor in. What came to pass was the most vigorous prayer meeting conceivable.

Nothing changed immediately. Our house was quarantined and I was taken, frightened and confused, to stay with an aunt. Nonetheless, we were all kept in perpetual prayer mode. Our church went into a season of fasting and prayer. After a few months, our Sunday school superintendent called. He told us that the entire church was joining Daisy's Sunday school class of nine-year-olds and would spend the day praying for a miracle.

Enter Jesus the healer!

At some miraculous moment during that sweet hour of prayer, Daisy's arms and legs suddenly began flailing. She was jubilant. "Mommy, Daddy," she shouted, "Come quick! Look! I'm healed!"[4]

Determined intercession released God's miraculous power. A meeting took place. *Paga* happened—God's power struck the mark. What a beautiful testimony!

The book of Acts has much to say about God's power being released through prayer. Chapter 2, verse 42 says, "They were continually devoting themselves to . . . prayer." What was the result? "Everyone kept feeling a sense of awe; and many wonders and signs were taking place through the apostles. And the Lord was adding to their number day by day those who were being saved" (Acts 2:43,47). Reverence, God's power and great harvest were all results of their intercession.

Again, in Acts 4:24, after some persecution began to occur, "they lifted their voices to God with one accord." Verse 31 gives the powerful result of this prayer: "And when they had prayed, the place where they had gathered together was shaken, and they were all filled with the Holy Spirit, and began to speak the word of God with boldness." Their prayers rose as incense to the throne and God literally shook the building as He poured forth His power. They were again filled with the Holy Spirit, and verse 33 adds that "with *great* power" they were demonstrating the resurrection of Christ. "Great" is the Greek word from which we get the English word "mega."[5] Intercession releases mega power!

Chapter six of Acts gives us another example of power released through prayer. The apostolic leaders of the church were becoming too busy with some of the practical administration of the church. Because of this, they were unable to spend the necessary time in prayer and study of the Word. This resulted in the appointing of the first deacons. "But we will devote ourselves to *prayer* and the ministry of the Word," the 12 apostles stated (Acts 6:4).

What was the result of this decision not to neglect prayer? Great harvest and power for the supernatural:

> And the word of God kept on spreading; and the number of the disciples continued to increase greatly in Jerusalem, and a great many of the priests were becoming obedient to the faith. And Stephen, full of grace and power, was performing great wonders and signs among the people (Acts 6:7-8).

The apostle Paul, whose ministry was built around much prayer and intercession, experienced the same results. In Acts 16:25-26, his worship and prayer produced an earthquake and a divine jailbreak. We're told in Acts 19:11-12 that God performed extraordinary miracles through him "so that handkerchiefs or aprons were even carried from his body to the sick, and the diseases left them and the evil spirits went out."

Does God do this sort of thing today? Absolutely. C. Peter Wagner shares the following story relayed to him by William Kumuyi, pastor of the Deeper Life Bible Church in Lagos, Nigeria, who has planted over 4,500 churches throughout Nigeria:

> At a regular Thursday night miracle meeting of an outlying Deeper Life Bible Church, the pastor asked all those who had sick people at home to hold up their handkerchiefs while he prayed a blessing of God's healing power upon them. They were to return home, place the handkerchief on the sick person, and pray for healing in Jesus' name. Unbeknownst to the pastor, the chief of a nearby Muslim village had come to visit the church that night—his first attendance at a Christian service. Although he didn't have anyone sick at home, he held up his handkerchief for the blessing.
>
> Soon after returning to his village, the chief attended the wake of a nine-year-old girl who had just died. While there, he suddenly remembered the handkerchief, retrieved it, placed it on the corpse, and prayed that she would be healed in Jesus' name. Then God did an obviously "unusual" miracle and raised the girl from the dead! The chief called an immediate ad hoc meeting with the village elders who had witnessed what had happened, then turned around and declared to his people: "For many years we have been serving Mohammed; but from this moment on our village will be a village of Jesus!" Needless to say, a Deeper Life Bible Church is now thriving in the village.[6]

Using the same methods today will produce the same results the Early Church experienced, because Christ is "the same yesterday and today, yes and forever" (Heb. 13:8). And the primary method of the Early Church was prayer.

Jane Rumph, in her book *Stories from the Front Lines*, tells of God releasing His power through intercession to actually heal a windmill. Yes, a windmill! As Rumph points out:

Although He generally chooses to operate according to the principles He established to govern the world, God has not stepped back passively from His creation and forsworn further involvement. The Lord, still sovereign over all He has made, can at any time set aside the laws of nature when doing so serves His higher purposes.[7]

Here is a shortened version of God's mechanical skills in the healing of the windmill:

Water was considered liquid gold in the barren desert region of northwestern Kenya, and the nomadic Turkana living there relied on the nearby windmill that pumped hundreds of gallons of water daily. When the water stopped flowing, it was of great concern to the entire community of Lorengalup. Randy Nelson and another missionary tried unsuccessfully to fix the windmill, but finally contacted the Kenyan contractor who had built it. He flew in from over four hundred miles away, discovered irreparable damage (probably caused by sand), and realized the entire pump had to be replaced. He returned home, intending to send a replacement pump, but was unable to find one.

Randy climbed to the top of the windmill and shut it down, locking the blades with a metal chain to prevent any further damage from occurring. He and his family then drove 460 miles to Nairobi, but were not able to locate a pump there, either. With no other solutions available, before leaving Nairobi, Randy contacted a colleague in the United States and asked him to bring a pump back with him when he returned in about ten days.

As the Nelsons approached Lorengalup on their return home, they were startled to realize that the blades of the windmill were rapidly spinning. As they pulled up to their home, a young Turkana man ran up to them, shouting the news that the windmill was once again pumping water. He went on to explain that while they were gone, some of the women had decided to pray for the windmill, just as the Nelsons had been teaching them to pray for the sick.

The Turkana women had gathered around the windmill, laid hands on it, and prayed for it to work. They continued in an intense time of intercession and worship. Shortly thereafter, a strong wind blew against the windmill, the metal chain broke, and the blades of the windmill began to turn. Upon checking the water tank, they rejoiced and praised God to see fresh water flowing out of the pipe. Randy was astounded that a broken pump that was unable to seal could be bringing water out of the ground. Yet that indeed was the case. The water continued to flow for the next few days, stopping just about the time the new pump arrived from the United States.

Today there are over a thousand nomadic Turkana believers, most of whom have heard the remarkable testimony of how the God who rules the universe answers prayers for personal needs and has no trouble healing a windmill.[8]

The intercession and worship of those dear Kenyans ascended as precious incense up to the throne of God. He was pleased with their childlike faith in His greatness and goodness, and as David said in Psalm 18:10, "He sped upon the wings of the wind," and healed the windmill. While the locals ironically called it a dust devil, this was actually a *paga* wind, released from the throne of God, which struck the mark with angelic accuracy and holy power!

The opposite of power is weakness or inability, which is what we have without the Holy Spirit's help. We're told in Romans 8:26-27:

And in the same way the Spirit also *helps* our *weakness*; for we do not know how to pray as we should, but the Spirit Himself intercedes for us with groanings too deep for words; and He who searches the hearts knows what the mind of the Spirit is, because He intercedes for the saints according to the will of God (emphasis added).

The word translated "weakness" literally means "an inability to produce results."[9] This certainly describes us in many situations. This passage says the Holy Spirit wants to help us in these situations. A more literal rendering of the word "helps" would be "taking hold of together with against."[10] The Holy Spirit wants to add His infinite power to our finite strength, giving us the results we need. This is well illustrated in the following story:

During heart surgery, a young wife and mother died on the operating table. She was finally resuscitated, but never regained consciousness. The doctors asserted that this was for the best, as her brain had been deprived of oxygen and would never again function properly. The pastor and others comforted the husband and prayed with him.

Three nights later, the pastor awakened, realized his wife wasn't in bed, and went to look for her. He found her lying on the living room floor, groaning. When he asked what was wrong, she said she didn't know, she didn't understand it, but she couldn't let the young woman die. For the next three nights, she lay on the floor, groaning and praying all night long.

On the following day, the woman in the hospital suddenly came to herself, amazing the doctors. Her mind was clear and she was perfectly fine. The Lord had restored her to her husband and children.

We must realize how dependent we are upon the Holy Spirit in our prayer lives. The pastor's wife entered into this time of intercession for the woman because the Spirit of God gave it to her—not because she worked it up.[11]

Notice how literally the verses in Romans were fulfilled through this situation. At times, the pastor's wife could only groan in intercession. This happens occasionally, when a burden from the Holy Spirit becomes so great that, not finding words to express it, the intercession of the Holy Spirit through us becomes groans or even deep weeping. Some would call this travail.[12]

At times words are simply not enough to convey the burden of our hearts. Should this happen to you, don't be alarmed. Simply pray—however the Holy Spirit directs—until you feel a release from the burden, or until the answer comes.

One other kind of intercession must be mentioned when we talk about power through prayer, for it results in a much greater release of power. This is the prayer of *agreement*. In Matthew 18:18-19, Jesus tells us:

> Truly I say to you, whatever you shall bind on earth shall be bound in heaven; and whatever you loose on earth shall be loosed in heaven. Again I say to you, that if two of you agree on earth about anything that they may ask, it shall be done for them by My Father who is in heaven.

Great power happens through unity. We move into a principle of multiplication, not addition. God told Israel, "Five of you will chase a hundred, and a hundred of you will chase ten thousand" (Lev. 26:8).

This principle of synergism is defined as "the combined action of two or more which have a greater total effect than the sum of their individual effects."[13] This term is used in the Scriptures to describe members of the Body of Christ functioning together.[14] In Romans 16:3, Philippians 1:24, and 3 John 1:8, the Holy Spirit tells us that the principle of synergism operates when we work together, and this certainly is true of prayer.

Gordon Lindsay, in his book *Prayer That Moves Mountains*, shares the following story of synergism created by the power of the prayer of agreement:

In May 1940 the Nazi Panzers advanced openly, and Britain appeared to be facing her worst defeat in history. The German High Command stated, "The British Army is encircled, and our troops are proceeding to its annihilation." In the natural, there was no hope. It seemed that hundreds of thousands of English boys would soon either be dead or suffering in Nazi prison camps.

A day of prayer was called by His Majesty the King on May 26th, and God came to the defense of His people! A storm descended in the area of Dunkirk, saving the armies from Nazi planes. Then God calmed the sea, allowing coastal yachts to transport troops from the beaches. The most optimistic hoped that twenty to thirty units could be saved; actually ten times that number were rescued.

The Daily Sketch declared, "Nothing like it ever happened before." Everywhere, the word "miracle" was spoken, as soldiers and civilians alike made mention of the *day of prayer*. Perhaps no one individual had faith for this miracle, but Christians united in prayer, as a king had faith to call the nation to prayer in their hour of distress. God answered and the nation was saved.[15]

When you are having difficulty breaking through or receiving victory in a difficult situation, find one or more believers to agree in prayer with you. Many times this is when the breakthrough comes. Five of the six testimonies shared in this chapter involved more than one person interceding for the situation. Don't try to fight adversity alone. Find someone to help you. God will respond to your prayers.

So often in our intercession, we forget that the power of the Holy Spirit is available to us. Don't make this mistake! If we cannot call upon the power of heaven, why are we praying at all? Remind yourself that you are calling upon an all-powerful God who intervenes in the affairs of Earth through the prayers of His people.

Ask for it. Believe lightning will fall, and the earth will shake. Your prayers are not earthbound; they arise before the throne of God as precious incense. His fire and power will be added, and together, you and God make an awesome team. You may never heal a windmill or raise the dead, but you can see changed lives, healed bodies, and the spiritually dead raised—all because you chose to partner with the God of thunder and lightning.

Let the storms begin!

Let's pray this prayer together:

Father, thank You for Your great love and awesome power. I need Your thunder and lightning to be released into [specify your need]. *I ask You to take hold of this situation with me. Help me in my inability to accomplish what is needed by demonstrating Your great strength. I know You work miracles today, Lord. Meet me with one in my time of need. I believe in Your great power and ask for it in Jesus' name.*
Amen.

Did You Understand?

1. How do thunder and lightning exemplify intercession?

2. What are some biblical examples of God's power being released through prayer?

3. What great truths can be seen in Romans 8:26-27?

4. What does synergy have to do with intercesion?

5. Don't you love studying God's Word?

Chapter Nine

The Perseverance of Intercession

I don't know why these things happen to me. Like the time I was expertly postulating on the subject of mind renewal in Detroit, Michigan. Saturday morning was the final four hours of a ten-hour course, and about three hours into this captivating dissertation one precious lady became overly mesmerized by the teaching. My words were bringing such peace to her troubled soul, she drifted off to sleep.

I don't like to brag, but not everyone can produce such mind-numbing revelation and soul-tranquilizing truth. Peace, that's what it is. It takes years of study and learning to mature to this point in public speaking.

To make this situation much more meaningful, this lady snored. The room wasn't all that big—there were probably 100 people seated around tables that each accommodated 8 to 10 people—and everyone was within earshot of this message-confirming endorsement of the highest order.

Her first snore wasn't all that great, just a small warm-up for those of us within 20 to 30 feet of her. Those seated next to her were gracious enough not to awaken her so that the full effect of this nasal applause could continue. Some would have foolishly roused her, robbing us of this blessing.

The second snore was better, becoming more worthy praise of such a glorious teaching, reaching two-thirds of the room. Those around her, appreciating the stunning effect these snorts of praise would produce, again allowed her to continue. I was amazed. Many people, unable to discern what was happening, would have nudged her awake.

The third snore reached full stature, the kind of zzzzzzzs dreams are made of—one for the record books—awakening everyone to the profoundness of my deep, stirring words. All eyes were on this peaceful woman.

"This," I shouted, seizing the moment, "is the kind of deep tranquility I'm speaking of. Let the power of my words so stir each of you. Hallelujah!"

The lady, awakened by my shouting, sat up with a start and grunted a loud "Amen!" which added increased weight to my words. Savoring the sweetness of the moment, I decided it was a good time for a coffee break. I could tell, by the smiles and soft chuckles, that everyone was greatly blessed.

A tape of this presentation, titled "Sounds of Serenity," can be ordered from my tape department.

Several years ago in Oklahoma, another lady helped me with one of my messages. I was commenting on the following verses: "That you may not be sluggish, but imitators of those who through faith and patience inherit the promises" (Heb. 6:12). "Therefore, do not throw away your confidence, which has a great reward. For you have need of endurance, so that when you have done the will of God, you may receive what was promised" (Heb. 10:35-36).

Making a strong point about the need for patience and endurance in order to receive answers to our prayers, I shared the following story.

One night a man had a dream in which he was being given a guided tour of heaven by an angel. He saw the golden streets, beautiful mansions, and millions of saints roaming this wonderful place.

Then he saw a huge building, miles long, which looked out of place. "What is that?" he asked the angel.

"That's God's warehouse," was the response. "It's where God stores the things He had prepared to give to people in answer to their prayers. Before He could release them, however, they gave up hope, lost their faith, and doubted His promise. Because their unbelief prohibited Him from distributing these things, He stores them in His warehouse."

"Wow!" said the man. "Can I see inside?"

"Sure," said the angel, and proceeded to show the man money, houses, cars, boats, clothing, food—just about everything you could think of—in this huge warehouse.

Just as I was about to make my powerful point—don't give up, casting away your confidence; you don't want your provision stored in God's heavenly warehouse—a little lady in the front row spoke up. In a pathetic, squeaky, fearful, almost tearful voice, she asked, "Were there any *men* there?"

I don't know if God has a warehouse, and if He does I doubt if there are any men there, but I do believe it is possible to ask God for something and fail to receive it because our faith wavered in the waiting time. *We need patience and perseverance in intercession. We must persevere in our praying and have patient endurance for our faith.*

Notice the warnings of Galatians 6:9 and James 1:6-7: "Let us not lose heart in doing good, for in due time we shall reap if we do not grow weary." "But let him ask in faith without any doubting, for the one who doubts is like the surf of the sea driven and tossed by the wind. *For let not that man expect that he will receive anything from the Lord*" (emphasis added).

The reaping in due time comes "if we do not grow weary." And "the one who doubts" shouldn't think "that he will receive anything from the Lord." This clearly tells us that we can fail to receive something we've asked God for, not because it isn't God's will to provide it, but because we did not persevere in believing or praying. I don't like this any more than you do, but we must acknowledge the truth of Scripture.

Persistence in prayer can mean persevering in one extended session of prayer, or persevering with many sessions over an extended season. On one occasion, Elijah persisted by praying seven times for rain. Though there were seven prayers, they were offered in one extended time of prayer (see 1 Kings 18:41-45). Daniel prayed for 21 days, several times a day, until the angel of the Lord broke through the warfare in the heavens with his answer (see Dan. 10). Jesus prayed three hours in the garden before He broke through and was able to face the cross (see Matt. 26:36-46).

I prayed for a young girl in a coma for an hour or two each week for a year before she was miraculously healed. I prayed an hour a day for a month before my wife was healed of an ovarian cyst. George Müller, an intercessor greatly used of God in the 1800s, testified that he knew of at least fifty thousand specific answers to his prayers, and had this to say about the necessity of persisting in prayer:

> The great point is never to give up until the answer comes. . . . The great fault of the children of God is that they do not continue in prayer; they do not go on praying; they do not persevere. If they desire anything for God's glory, they should pray until they get it. Oh, how good, kind, gracious, and generous is the One with whom we have to do![1]

Müller prayed for a man's salvation for 63 years! The man received Christ after Müller's death, standing over Müller's grave. Persistence won again!

Through binoculars, the Ring Nebula, in the constellation Lyra, looks like a smoke ring. Actually a star in the process of exploding, its light first reached the earth in 1054. It was a supernova then, and so bright it shone in the daytime. Though not as bright now, it is still exploding and expanding at the rate of seventy million miles a day. It is interesting to look at something expanding at this rate, and not see it budge. Its apparent size does not increase. Photographs taken fifteen years ago seem identical to current photographs of it.

The process of prayer often resembles this nebula. Huge happenings are not always visible to the naked eye—especially in the spiritual realm. Sometimes we pray and pray and seemingly see no change. But that's only true from our perspective.

If we could see from heaven's standpoint, we would know what God is doing and intending to do. We would see God working in hearts in ways we cannot know. We would see God orchestrating circumstances about which we know nothing. We would see a galaxy of details being set in place for the moment when God brings the answer to fulfillment.[2]

Yes, continued, persistent prayer is necessary. But why? We are much more apt to do something—especially something difficult, which persisting prayer is—if we understand why it is necessary. Why must we persist in prayer? What causes delays in answers to prayer?

First, let me explain what is NOT happening as we persist in prayer. We are not talking God into doing something. We are not changing His will. First John 5:14-15 tells us, "And this is the confidence which we have before Him, that, if we ask anything *according to His will*, He hears us. And if we know that He hears us in whatever we ask, we know that we have the requests which we have asked from Him" (emphasis added).

We are to ask for that which is in agreement with God's revealed will in Scripture. Therefore, our persistence is not to overcome a hesitancy or reluctance on His part. We must always remember that we are dealing with an all-wise God. He does not have to think about something for a while, trying to figure out what is right, or whether or not He should give it to us.

Yet, there are times in Scripture when intercession or changes of heart in people caused God to change His *mind* on something. Abraham's intercession for Sodom, Moses' intercession for Israel, and Ninevah's repentance all caused God to change His *plans* (see Gen. 18:20-33; Exod. 32:7-14; Jon. 3:4-10). It is important to realize, however, that God's *will* and *heart* never changed in these situations.

What was really happening? As a righteous and holy God, He must judge sin. He is also love, however, and as such desires to forgive and redeem. As we pointed out in chapter 2, He works through people—our prayers, actions, and the like—and has greatly limited Himself in this decision. When He can find someone through whom to work, His will is accomplished. When He is unable to find someone, His will in that situation is often frustrated.

The above examples—Abraham, Moses and Ninevah—show us that God's holiness demanded judgment, but His desire was forgiveness. His *mind* or *plans* were changed by prayer, not His *will*.

What, then, are the reasons for delays in answers to prayer, causing us to have to persist in intercession and faith? First of all, God's perfect timing is always an element. Three words in the New Testament describe different stages of time. One involves time in general,[3] another strategic or opportune time[4]—a window of opportunity, for example—and the third is a word meaning the fullness of time.[5]

The Scriptures tell us that Jesus was born at the fullness of time (see Gal. 4:4). Although it was many years after the fall of humankind, God, in His infinite wisdom, knows the perfect timing for all things. He waited until the right moment in history to send Christ to Earth.

Hannah, a barren woman in Israel, waited several years for God to answer her prayers for a child (see 1 Sam. 1).

At the right time, however, God gave her a son, Samuel, who became a great prophet in Israel. God not only wanted to answer her prayer, but also to meet His need for a prophet. I'm sure she questioned the delay, but history gives us the reason.

The same could be said of the birth of John the Baptist. His mother, Elizabeth, was also barren. God waited many years to answer her and Zacharias's desire for children, in order to bring him into the world at just the right time (see Luke 1:5-25). I'm sure they questioned why, but God had a "fullness" of time.

Abraham and Sarah waited 25 years for the fulfillment of God's promise to give them a son. They had to wait for God's perfect time (see Gen. 12:1-7; 21:1-5). Not only did this fulfill God's plans, but I'm sure it also worked character and other qualities into them. James 1:3 tells us, "The testing of your faith produces endurance."

This leads to the second reason for delays in answers to prayer. Often God can teach us truths and build our characters during the waiting time in ways that no other process could accomplish. When I spent a year praying for the young girl in a coma, God taught me many things, not the least of which was patience or endurance. He also increased my compassion for people who were hurting during this time. He taught me the power of certain forms of prayer and that they often work together. There are simply some things God can work into us during periods of waiting and persevering that He can do no other way.

A common sight in America's Southwest desert is the century plant. It's unique. The century plant

(*Agave Americana*) thrives in rocky, mountainous, desert sites. It has dramatic, splayed leaves that grow up to a foot wide. The plant can reach twelve feet in diameter.

But what makes the century plant unusual, as its name suggests, is its long reproduction cycle. For twenty or thirty years (no, not a literal one hundred years), the six-foot-tall plant stands the same height and puts out no flowers. Then, one year, without warning, a new bud sprouts. The bud, which resembles a tree-trunk-size asparagus spear, shoots into the sky at a fantastic rate of seven inches per day and reaches an eventual height of twenty to forty feet. Then it crowns itself with several clumps of yellowish blossoms that last up to three weeks.

Like the century plant, many of the most glorious things that happen to us come only after a long wait.[6]

A third reason for delays in answers to prayer is the need for God to work in others who may be a part of the answer. For example, if our intercession is for the salvation of other people, it can take time—sometimes a lot of time—for God to be able to change their hearts and desires. If I'm praying for someone else's deliverance from habits or other strongholds, it may take God a while to bring that person to the level of understanding needed to change, just as it did with the man for whom Müller prayed for 63 years. Simply stated, circumstances often prohibit God from answering a prayer quickly.

Epaphras "labored" in prayer for the Colossians to mature in their walk with Christ (see Col. 4:12). Maturing takes time. Epaphras knew this and persevered—labored—in his intercession.

Finally, when our intercession is releasing the power of the Holy Spirit to overcome the powers of darkness, this often takes time. Although he may not have been aware of it, the biblical character Daniel was involved in "warfare" while interceding for Israel's restoration. His prayers were affecting the spiritual realm, where a great battle was taking place between angels and demons. Angels were dispatched to answer his prayers, but demonic powers were hindering them (see Dan. 10:12-13). The issue wasn't whether or not God could overpower Satan's kingdom—He certainly can—but whether or not there would be enough involvement (prayer), humanly speaking, to release that power. Again, God works through people, and Daniel was the person in this instance.

Paul Billheimer, in his great book *Destined for the Throne*, says of Daniel's intercession:

> Daniel evidently realized that intercession had a part to play in bringing the prophecy to pass. God had made the prophecy. *When it was time for its fulfillment He did not fulfill it arbitrarily outside of His program of prayer. He sought for a man upon whose heart He could lay a burden of intercession. . . . As always, God made the decision in heaven. A man was called upon to enforce that decision on earth through intercession and faith.*[7]

Jane Rumph shares the following story of persevering intercession that, over an extended period of time, broke through the enemy's strongholds:

The spiritual battle over Sri Kuncoro in Indonesia was fought for many years. Although known as a center of prostitution, a local pastor was not willing to relinquish this ground to Satan, and organized "prayer drives." Month after month, year after year, intercessors gathered for praise and worship before spending the rest of the night praying on-site at various points to which they had driven, throughout the city. These prayer warriors bound the demonic spirits and declared the deception over this area to be broken through the authority of Christ. They cried out for the residents to be freed from the enemy's grasp and to receive Jesus Christ as their Lord and Savior.

While there were no apparent changes in the natural realm, in the spiritual realm the continued intercessory blows of these faithful people cracked the enemy's strongholds. Years later, the invisible walls of darkness were crushed when a resident of Sri Kuncoro was dramatically healed of tuberculosis and years of paralysis. This man and his family became Christians, and the neighbors, astounded at his miraculous healing, also came to God. The report of this miracle spread, and, within a couple of years, fifty new converts had been baptized.[8]

As seen in this story, a miracle can bring widespread results. In Acts 9:32-35, we read of such an experience in Peter's ministry:

> Now it came about that as Peter was traveling through all those parts, he came down also to the saints who lived at Lydda. And there he found a certain man named Aeneas, who had been bedridden eight years, for he was paralyzed. And Peter said to him, "Aeneas, Jesus Christ heals you; arise, and make your bed." And immediately he arose. And all who lived at Lydda and Sharon saw him, and they turned to the Lord.

When an entire city or region comes to Christ after a single healing, the possibility exists that the miracle shattered an invisible demonic barrier. Second Corinthians 4:4 says, "The god of this age has blinded the minds of unbelievers, so that they cannot see the light of the gospel of the glory of Christ, who is the image of God." When these blinders are ripped off of unbelievers' minds by the power of God, they are then able to see the truth clearly as never before, and can understand and respond to the gospel. This often takes time, just as it did in Sri Kuncoro. The miracle that brought the breakthrough came after months of consistent intercession.

I mentioned praying for my wife, Ceci, for 30 days for the healing of an ovarian cyst. We knew from her symptoms and doctor's reports that the cyst was shrinking throughout that process. The power of the Holy Spirit was being released consistently to heal her, but we believe

my prayers were releasing that power. The Lord had chosen not to do it as an instant miracle, which is often the
case, but through power continually released by persistent intercession.

> When Dwight Eisenhower was a young boy, he fell
> and injured his leg. Within a couple of days he could
> no longer walk, and became bedridden. When the
> doctor examined the leg, he said the infection was so
> serious that he didn't think the leg could be saved.
> Dwight insisted his leg not be cut off, and, because
> his parents weren't completely convinced that am-
> putation was necessary, they did not follow the doc-
> tor's recommendation. As the doctor had predicted,
> Dwight's condition became more critical—his fever
> increased and the infection spread up his leg. The
> doctor was extremely frustrated that the parents
> weren't heeding his advice, and told them the life
> of their son was in their hands. The Eisenhowers,
> remembering their faith in God and their minister's
> belief in healing through faith, began a bedside vigil
> of prayer for Dwight. Each family member took
> turns, so that someone was always beside him, pray-
> ing for his healing. Upon his return, the doctor was
> amazed to see the improvement in Dwight's condi-
> tion. The life of Dwight Eisenhower was saved, and
> he later became the president of the United States
> of America.[9]

It cannot be proven that the Eisenhower family's continued intercession was releasing power to heal Dwight,

but it certainly is a reasonable explanation. A word of caution should be given here. I believe God works through doctors and medicine. Usually the wisest decision is to follow their advice. Much confirmation and the counsel of mature spiritual leaders should be sought before a decision such as the one the Eisenhowers made is chosen.

The Lord instructs us not to "lose heart" in our prayer efforts: "And let us not lose heart in doing good, for in due time we shall reap if we do not grow weary" (Gal. 6:9). The Greek word used for "lose heart" means to lose one's courage and become fainthearted. It is used in the sense of being in the midst of misfortune or a desperate situation. Paul used it twice in 2 Corinthians 4:1,16 to describe the difficulties he suffered in his apostolic ministry. He was stoned, beaten, shipwrecked and rejected, and suffered numerous other hardships, but he was determined not to lose heart or give up. When facing difficulties and delays in our intercession, we must reach deep into our spirits for the endurance provided by the Holy Spirit, and make sure we do not lose heart.

Mount Blanc, the highest peak in the Alps, is tremendously difficult to climb. Those who attempt it must carry only the barest essentials. One man disdained this wisdom and carried his "essentials": notebooks, wine, delicacies, a special cap, a colorful blanket, and a camera. As he climbed, these "essentials" lost their value and were abandoned along the wayside. He reached the top, but only after giving up everything not truly essential—his interpretation of "essential" had drastically changed.

A teacher once compared this to his life: "When young, food, clothing, and full records of my experiences to impress the world were important. At forty, only clothing that kept me warm mattered; at fifty, I only needed food that made me strong. At sixty, my 'climb' became so steep that I only wanted to reach the top—the opinions of others meant nothing."

Many people, realizing the cumbersomeness of their "essentials," decide to forgo the peak and settle for a lesser place where they can be comfortable with their plans and accessories. How much better to consider Jesus! He relinquished everything that hindered to fulfill God's plan. We must also do this to fully accomplish that which is set before us.[10]

There have been many prayer "climbs" that I have considered abandoning. I wasn't sure if I had the time, energy and discipline to continue. When I chose to press on, however, I realized that to finish my climb I had to abandon some nonessentials: TV, certain pleasures, at times even a meal or two. When I reached the top—the answered prayer—I realized how unimportant those other things were.

Prayer takes time. It requires energy. Often it is simply the spiritual discipline of persistence that makes the difference. We in America have developed a "now" mentality. We have been wonderfully spoiled to the conveniences of our culture, be they microwaves or fast food. There are situations, however, when the only solution is to slow down, take our time, and determine that we are going to go the distance. Life is a marathon, not a sprint. Most of the time, so is intercession. Decide now, once and for all, that you are a "stayer."

See you at the top!

Let's pray this prayer together:

> *Father, I know You have a fullness of time for my situation. I pray that You give me the strength to persevere and to not lose heart and give up. I know You are working Your character into me as I wait, and I thank You for that.*
>
> *I want to be like Daniel of old, who persisted through the warfare and caused the battle in the heavens to be won by the forces of righteousness. Like Hannah, I not only want my needs to be met, but I want Your purposes to be fulfilled as well. Help me to always be a stayer, releasing the fruit of perseverance.*
>
> *In Jesus' name, I ask.*
>
> *Amen.*

Did You Understand?

1. Is it possible to ask God for something in faith and still not receive the answer? What verses give proof of this?

2. Does God's will change because of our prayers? Explain.

3. What are the three types of timing in Scripture? How do they relate to intercession?

4. Do other people sometimes cause delays to our prayers? How can this be?

5. Do you have anything "stored" in heaven?

Chapter Ten

Proactive Intercession

I played high school football for a small, country school. I was a small quarterback, and I had small linemen who threw lots of "look out" blocks: "Look out, Dutch!" The results were predictable: a broken nose, a separated shoulder, a bum knee, nine stitches under my eye, bruised ribs, two major concussions, backaches today from a slightly twisted rib cage, and *brain damage*!

I developed great reflexes, the ability to *react* quickly to sadistic defensive linemen and linebackers who received stars on their helmets and eventual scholarships for giving small quarterbacks broken noses, separated shoulders, bum knees . . . you get the picture.

Too often we're *reactionary* where Satan is concerned. The results? You guessed it: breaks, bruises, separations, and various other spiritual casualties. We must learn to be *proactive* in our intercession, not waiting for Satan's attacks and then *reacting*, but *proactively* praying against the stealing, killing and destroying of the "thief" (see John 10:10).

This describes a concept of prayer known as watchman intercession.[1] Isaiah 62:6 says, "On your walls, O Jerusalem, I have appointed watchmen; all day and all night they will never keep silent. You who remind the Lord, take no rest for yourselves."

Two New Testament Scriptures also mention the watching aspect of intercession. The first is Ephesians 6:18: "With all prayer and petition pray at all times in the Spirit, and with this in view, *be on the alert* with all perseverance and petition for all the saints" (emphasis added). The *King James Version* uses the word "watching" for the phrase "be on the alert."

The second verse is 1 Peter 5:8: "Be of sober spirit, *be on the alert*. Your adversary, the devil, prowls about like a roaring lion, seeking someone to devour" (emphasis added). Again, other translations use the word "watchful." The context of both verses is spiritual warfare. Each mentions our adversary and challenges us to alertness or watchfulness, both for ourselves and for our brothers and sisters in Christ.

Too often Christians have interpreted these verses as only reactive—in other words, waiting for the attack and then going into damage control. While intercession can certainly release God's redemption into destructive situations, God is offering us much more than "look-out blocks" and damage control. He desires to warn us *in advance* of Satan's attacks so that we can pray for others and build the boundaries of protection we spoke of in chapter 7. This is watchman intercession.

I do not mean to imply that every negative thing that happens to people is a direct result of Satan. I realize that our own carelessness, the carelessness of others, the curse of sin on our fallen world, and other causes all result in accidents, disease and other destructive events. I believe there is protection from both satanic attacks and otherwise-caused adversity to be found through watchman intercession.

The Old Testament Hebrew words translated "watchman" or "watching" have the basic connotation of protecting or preserving through attentive watching.[2] The New Testament Greek words have the same implied meanings, though their literal meanings are "being awake" or "sleepless," as in sentries or night watchmen.[3] The following story exemplifies the watchman concept.

Aglow International was holding its annual conference in Denver, Colorado, in 1992, when Cindy Jacobs interrupted the meeting with a strong SOS warning she had just received from the Lord for Bob Byerly, Jim and Bobbye Byerly's son. Bobbye, then the national president of Aglow International, was on the platform. Bob was, and still is, a police officer in the Denver area. Cindy explained the urgency and seriousness of what she was sensing, and then led those present in a powerful time of intercession for Bob's immediate safety—for God to protect him against the attacks of the enemy.

Bobbye spoke later with her son and found out what had happened that evening. When he responded to a suicide threat, a man who declared that he wanted to kill a cop shot at him and another officer. Thankfully, the bullets went over their heads, and they escaped injury. A potentially tragic event had been averted as people had heeded the strategic warning of the Holy Spirit and prayed for Bob's immediate protection.

That is proactive, watching intercession!

Second Corinthians 2:11 is a great verse that sheds wonderful light on our subject: "In order that no advantage be taken of us by Satan; for we are not ignorant of his schemes." The word "ignorant" means "to be without knowledge or understanding."[4] The word "schemes" literally means "thoughts," but also has come to mean "plans, schemes, plots and devices," as these things are born in the thoughts of the mind.[5]

This verse shows us that God doesn't want us to be without knowledge or understanding of the way the enemy thinks and operates—of his plans, plots, schemes and devices. Therefore, we can assume that He is willing to reveal them to us. He certainly wanted the Body of Christ to have knowledge of the enemy's plot against Bob Byerly in October 1992. The Lord gave Cindy Jacobs the understanding of the immediate need for prayer, she alerted those present, the watchman aspect of intercession took place, and the enemy's plan failed.

What if they had been unaware of Satan's schemes that night? The enemy could have taken advantage of Bob. The word "advantage" means "to have or hold the greater portion." Other meanings include "to make a prey of, to defraud, and to make a gain."[6] Satan makes a lot of gains on those who are unaware of his ways.

Let's look at this verse again with all of these concepts included: "To the degree we are ignorant of the way our adversary thinks and operates—of his plans, plots, schemes and devices—to that degree he will gain on us, prey on us, defraud us of what is ours, and have or hold the greater portion."

The greater portion of what? Whatever! Our homes, marriages, families, communities, money, government, nation, and more. Twenty-five years ago the Church in America was without understanding of what Satan was planning, and he got the greater portion of our schools.

The same could be said of our government and many of our churches!

I want to draw four conclusions from the three verses we've used—Ephesians 6:18, 1 Peter 5:8, and 2 Corinthians 2:11:

1. *Protection from the attacks of our enemy—even for believers—is not automatic.* There is a part for us to play. Though God is sovereign, this does not mean He is literally in control of everything that happens. He has left much to the decisions and actions of humankind. If God were going to protect or safeguard us from Satan's attacks regardless of what we did, these verses would be totally irrelevant to Christians. Somewhere in our theology, we must find a place for human responsibility. At some point we must begin to believe that we matter, that we're relevant, for ourselves and for others.

2. *God's plan is to warn or alert us to Satan's tactics.* This is deduced from the simple fact that, since God says not to be unaware of Satan's tactics, He must be willing to make us aware of them. If He says to be on the alert, this must mean that if we are, He will alert us. God wouldn't ask of us something He wasn't also going to enable us to accomplish.

3. *We must be alert—remain watchful—or we won't be aware of God's attempts to warn us of Satan's attacks and plans.* If these attacks were always going to

be obvious, alertness wouldn't be necessary. Isaiah 56:10 speaks of blind watchmen. What a picture! I'm afraid it has been a fairly good description of many of us in our watching roles. We're often like the disciples of old: We have eyes, but we do not see (see Mark 8:18). It's time we do more than gaze; we must alertly watch!

4. *If we are not alert and watchful, if we are ignorant of Satan's schemes, he will take the bigger portion.* He will gain on us, taking advantage of our ignorance. Contrary to popular belief, we really can be destroyed due to ignorance (see Hos. 4:6).[7]

The good news is that God does not intend for Satan to take advantage of us. He will alert us to his schemes, if we pay attention and remain alert. Adam, the first watchman in the Bible, failed in this. In Genesis 2:15, God told Adam to "keep" the garden. The word "keep," though not translated as such here, also comes from one of the three Hebrew words for "watchman." Adam had been assigned to protect the garden, watching for attacks from Satan. He was not alert as he should have been, and therefore Satan "took advantage" of him and Eve.

This first use of the term "watchman" gives us a clear picture of the role of watchmen: to keep the serpent out of our gardens (our homes, families, churches and cities).

In *First Things First*, A. Roger Merrill tells of a business consultant who decided to landscape his grounds. He hired a woman with a doctorate in horticulture who was extremely knowledgeable.

Because the business consultant was very busy and traveled a lot, he kept emphasizing to her the need to create his garden in a way that would require little or no maintenance on his part. He insisted on automatic sprinklers and other labor-saving devices. Finally she stopped and said, 'There's one thing you need to deal with before we go any further. If there's no gardener, there's no garden!' "[8]

The following story illustrates how a watching intercessor prayed and kept her "garden" safe during one of the most infamous events in history:

One Sunday in April 1912, the *Titanic* struck an iceberg. Colonel Gracy, a passenger on the ship, after helping launch the few lifeboats that were available, had resigned himself to death. However, as he slipped beneath the waves, his wife at home was suddenly awakened with great concern for her husband. She prayed for several hours, until peace came. Meanwhile, Gracy bobbed to the surface near a capsized boat and eventually was rescued. He and his wife later discovered that during the very hours she was agonizing in prayer, he was clinging desperately to this overturned boat.[9]

Notice that Mrs. Gracy was alert—she was watching. Her warning came simply as a "concern," which many people would have ignored or tried not to worry about. Second, as He promised He would if we're alert, God was faithful to give the warning. Third, she prayed until peace came. This means she didn't simply make a quick request, but continued to pray until the concern left and the peace of God came in its place.

Studying other ways in which the Hebrew words for "watchman" are translated and used will add further insight to watching intercession.

"Keep" or "keeper" is far and away the most frequent usage of the word. Related translations are "preserve" and "maintain." When God asked Cain where his brother Abel was, knowing full well he had murdered him, Cain's reply was, "Am I my brother's *keeper*?" (Gen. 4:9). The right answer is yes, though Cain was implying otherwise.

Jesus was a *keeper* of Peter in Luke 22:31-32: "Simon, Simon, behold, Satan has demanded permission to sift you like wheat; but I have prayed for you, that your faith may not fail; and you, when once you have turned again, strengthen your brothers." Though Peter denied Christ, his calling was *preserved* or *maintained* by Christ's intercession for him. It is reasonable to assume, based on Christ's words, that had Christ not been a watchman for him, Peter would not have been saved.

We can be *keepers* today. We can *preserve* lives, destinies, health, ministries, and more through our intercession. When warnings are heard and acted upon, the interloping serpent is kept from our gardens. Security is maintained.

We do this for ourselves, as well as for others. Elmer Towns recalls an experience where God protected him from harm:

> At the conclusion of a seminar in California, instead of pronouncing a benediction to close the meeting, Towns asked the people to kneel by their

chairs while he prayed. He knelt at the end chair of the first row, near a window. After dedicating the people to God's service, he prayed the Lord's Prayer, paraphrasing it to apply to those in attendance that day. He concluded his prayer this way: "Deliver us from the evil one who would hurt us in ways we don't even think about." As he arose and walked back to the lectern, the nearby ornate Spanish window fell from its casing and suddenly crashed onto the chair he had just left. Shattered glass was everywhere, and the heavy frame had smashed right over the area where Towns had just been kneeling. It's impossible to know what might have happened to him, had he not moved when he did.[10]

Towns, though not necessarily alerted in advance to this potential accident, has made a practice of praying daily the phrase from the Lord's Prayer, "Deliver us from the evil one." This is an important aspect of proactive watchman prayer. We shouldn't assume that we need to pray only when warned. Jesus told us to pray daily for deliverance from the evil one. I believe Towns's consistent prayer for himself allowed God to protect him from this bizarre accident.

Another usage of the words for "watchman" is "pay attention" or "listen." This should be fairly obvious. If we are to hear or discern the warnings of the Holy Spirit, we must be listening for them. Some would teach that God no longer speaks to us, but nowhere do the Scriptures support this. If this were the case, verses such as those mentioned earlier in the chapter—1 Peter 5:8, Ephesians 6:18, and 2 Corinthians 2:11—would make no sense.

Certainly, the "voice" of the Lord comes to us in various ways—Scriptures that are made alive to us; premonitions; thoughts that originate with God; others sharing verses or God-inspired thoughts with us; and the still, small voice of the Lord—but it certainly comes. If we're listening, that is.

Cindy Jacobs, in *The Voice of God*, shares a story Shirley Dobson told of praying for her daughter, Danae:

> I was at home one rainy weekend and looking forward to working on several projects I had set aside for just such a time. Both Jim and Ryan [their son] were in Northern California on a hunting trip, and Danae had plans for the evening with one of her friends. She had previously asked for permission to use the family car for her outing.
>
> Secretly happy to have some time to myself, I turned on some music and was busy at work when suddenly a heaviness descended upon me. Feelings of unexplainable anxiety and fear for Danae washed over me. I thought, *This is silly. She's out with her friend, having a good time. I'm sure she is all right.* Instead of lessening, the apprehension I felt grew more intense. Finally, I slipped into the bedroom, closed the door, and got down on my knees.
>
> "Lord," I prayed, "I don't know why I am experiencing such fear about Danae, but if she is in any danger, I ask You to send guardian angels to watch over, protect, and bring her home safely."

I continued praying for a time and then got up and went back to work. The burden lifted to some degree, but I still sensed an uneasiness.

Forty-five minutes later I heard a knock on the door. Opening it, I found a policeman standing on my porch. He asked me if I owned a red car, and I replied in the affirmative. "I found it upside down on a mountain road, Mrs. Dobson. Who was driving? Was it your husband?" he questioned. Danae had been driving the red car. I now realized why the Lord had impressed me to pray. Later I was to realize just how powerful that time of intercession on her behalf had been.

While he [the policeman] was there, the hospital emergency room called. They wouldn't tell me details. I found Danae very shaken, with her left hand badly injured, swollen and bleeding. She had used her left arm and hand to brace herself as the car rolled over, and the car had actually rolled on her hand. We were told she could have lost her hand had her palm been facing down. Fortunately, a noted hand surgeon was in the hospital that night and was able to operate immediately. Another answer to prayer.

Later, we were to learn the whole story. Even though she had been driving very slowly, the rain had washed gravel over the oil-slick road, causing her to skid as she rounded the curve. She became very scared and lost control, as most young drivers would. The car landed upside down in the middle of the road. If she had gone another thirty feet, the car would have plunged off the road and down a five-hundred-foot embankment. There was no guardrail. With much gratitude in my heart, I thought about my prayer in light of the accident and saw legions of angels lined up against the road, keeping her car from sliding over the edge. Another answer to prayer! Danae quickly recovered, regaining full use of her left hand, and we give much praise to the Lord.[11]

I was ministering in Toronto several months ago. My last morning there, as I was packing my bags and thinking about my final session, I was also visiting with the Holy Spirit. I wasn't in intercession, and this wasn't during my quiet time. I was simply communing while working, sharing some of my inner thoughts with Him, much the same way I might have done with my wife, had she been there.

Suddenly He spoke to me. It was as natural and matter of fact as if two friends were sharing their hearts. "Japan is really on My heart this morning," the Holy Spirit said. This surprised me because I've never thought about God having one place on His heart more than others. I've always figured He had *every place* on His heart all the time. And the phrase "on My heart" surprised me as well. It was more than on His mind; this was something deeper—very important to Him. I felt as though He was letting me into His very heart.

He then said to me, "I must have Japan. It is a gate to Asia and I must have it. There is tremendous warfare over the nation right now. Would you pray for Japan this morning in your session?"

How do you like that?! Not a command, "Pray for Japan," but a question, "Would you?" He was *asking* me!

"Of course we will, Holy Spirit," I said. "We would be honored to do that." And we did! Such an anointing and burden came upon the assembly . . . tears . . . travail . . . intense intercession. It went on for about 45 minutes, at which time I had to leave for the airport. They continued—how long I do not know.

In that session, God brought us tremendous insight into how to pray for Japan. He spoke to us prophetically some promises to lay hold of and declare over the nation. It was glorious. I'm told that, through some Japanese who were in that session, other believers in Japan have heard about this, and they have been very encouraged. Japan will be saved! (I'm not implying this only because of our prayers in Toronto. Many others have, no doubt, also prayed effectively for Japan. But due to the strong witness in my heart that day, I have great faith concerning this nation.)

This watching and subsequent intercession was born out of fellowship with the Holy Spirit. As we spend time communing with Him, which involves listening as well as talking, we grow more sensitive to His promptings.

The three Old Testament words for "watchman" are also translated "protector," "guard" or "bodyguard." One of the most astounding stories illustrating this facet of watching intercession is shared by my dear friend Beth Alves:

An example from my own life involves a favorite cousin I hadn't seen in about ten years. I had crawled out of bed in the middle of the night for a glass of water when a picture of my cousin canvassed my mind. Suddenly I dropped to my knees and began to cry out, "God, don't let Mike move! Keep him still, Lord! Keep him still! Oh God, please don't let him move! Hold him, Lord! Hold him!"

Even though I was pleading on Mike's behalf with my words, I remember thinking, *This is really ridiculous. Why am I praying this?* Then the words ceased, and when they did, I could not muster another word. So I got up, drank a glass of water, and started back toward the bedroom. Again I fell to the floor and began to cry out with a grave sense of urgency. "Don't let him move, God! Don't let Mike move! Stay still! Stay still!" The words came to an abrupt end. This time I thought, *Oh, no! This must be a nightmare!*

I had no feeling inside of me other than the need to pray. I got up and began to pace the floor, wondering what in the world this was all about. One more time I took a few steps toward the bedroom, and again I dropped to the floor. Only this time I was yelling, "Get him up, Lord! Get him to run! Run, Mike! Lord, help him to run . . . run . . . run! Let him run, God! Run, run, run!" After several minutes, a calm came over me and I returned to bed for the night.

The following day, I called my aunt to see if she could help me put the pieces together about my puzzling outcries the night before. She informed me that Mike was in Vietnam. The experience still made very little sense.

Finally, a month later, my aunt called to read a letter she had received. The letter told how Mike, who was a pilot, had been shot down and landed in a tree. He had been warned to get out of the area as quickly as possible, but explained that just a few hundred yards from the crash site, he fell into a bush. "Mom," he wrote, "it was like I was pinned down. I felt like somebody was sitting on me. The Vietcong came and were unknowingly standing on my pant leg while looking up at my parachute in the tree. They turned around and began to slash the bushes with their bayonets. It looked safe, so I started to get up and was about to run when once again I fell into the bush as though someone were pushing me. I lay there for a couple of minutes until suddenly I had an impulse to get up and run. I heard a helicopter so I sprinted through the wooded area, following the direction of the noise, to an open space where I was whisked off to safety. The helicopter crew said they came in response to my beeper. And yet, it had not been working when I was shot down." That, dear ones, is intercession![12]

One more fitting meaning of the watchman in the Old Testament was "doorkeeper" or "gatekeeper." Watchmen determine through prayer what comes into their lives, homes, churches, cities and nations. They refuse to allow entrance to the serpent or any of his emissaries.

An example of gatekeeping for a nation began when I took my daughter Sarah on a prayer journey to Washington,

D.C., in August 1999, for her thirteenth birthday. She and my other daughter, Hannah, are becoming true intercessors. While praying with me on the Washington Mall, Sarah said, "Dad, I believe we're supposed to come back and pray here again with several more teens and their parents. I feel we're to do this before The Call to help prepare the way for this event through intercession."

(The Call DC was a gathering of four hundred thousand youth and adults—mostly youth—on the Washington Mall in our nation's capital on September 2, 2000. The purpose of the event was to be a day of prayer and fasting to repent and pray for revival in America. Many of those attending participated in 40 days of fasting leading up to the event. It was an awesome occasion, a true history maker.)

Two or three more times over the next few months, Sarah repeated this. She was emphatic, "We must do this, Dad."

"Okay," I said. "We'll do it."

We set the trip for late June 2000, and several other families from our fellowship planned to join us. A few months before the time came, I received a call from some friends in Spokane, Washington, saying they were taking a team of intercessors to D.C. for the same purpose as we were—*at the same time!* They were wondering if I would be willing to join them and speak during a service on the Mall.

"Sure, I was already planning to be there!" I responded.

When the journey actually took place, we had incredible times of prayer in our nation's capital, but the highlight was a service on the Mall on Sunday morning. As it turned out, the Dalai Lama of the Buddhist religion was scheduled to lead a service on the other end of the Mall at the same time as ours. His was for the purpose of calling over 700 demonic spirits into our nation for the propagation of the Buddhist religion.

In the sovereign plan of God, we were placed between him and the Capitol Building. We knew immediately upon hearing about it that God had placed us there as gatekeepers to protect our nation's capital from these evil spirits.

We were later informed that the Dalai Lama had to apologize to the people. Though he tried, he just couldn't get these spirits summoned, it seemed. We know why. The gate was closed!

A group of intercessors in the state of Washington and a 13-year-old girl in Colorado had heard the call to go to Washington, D.C., and pray. Though we didn't have a specific warning about what was going to happen that day, we felt the prompting of the Holy Spirit to go. The rest is history.

We must learn to listen to the Holy Spirit. He will guide us in our intercession and alert us to the schemes of the enemy. We need not allow the serpent into our gardens. To the contrary, as it says in Luke 10:19, we can "tread upon serpents and scorpions, and over all the power of the enemy."

Let's go tend our gardens!

Let's pray this prayer together:

Father, I accept Your assignment in my life to keep the serpent out of my garden. His schemes will not succeed against my home and family. I stand now as a doorkeeper for my children [or whatever your garden may be], and I say no compromise will come into their lives. No attempt to harm them will succeed. I claim Your promise that they will be taught by You and great will be their peace. I ask You to establish them in righteousness and to keep them far from oppression and fear (see Isa. 54:13-14).

Holy Spirit, as I listen to You, help me to be sensitive to Your voice. Alert me to Satan's schemes and plans. Don't allow the serpent to take advantage of my family in any way. Thank You, Father, for these things.

I ask them in Jesus' name,
Amen.

Did You Understand?

1. How important is it for us to be aware of the enemy's schemes? Why?

2. List some of the ways we can function as watchman intercessors.

3. How can we become more sensitive to the Holy Spirit's promptings?

4. Has God given you a garden to tend?

Chapter Eleven

Proclamation Intercession

It was 1980 and I was fresh out of Bible school. I was radical enough spiritually to pray for anything that moved—or grew. That's why I was standing in the middle of a field, reading the Bible to the crops.

Now that I have your attention . . . No, I'm not kidding. And I don't think I'm crazy, either. I was taking my cue from Jesus, who spoke to a tree on one occasion. He spoke a death sentence to it, and the next day it was dead (see Mark 11:13-14,20).

He also spoke to a storm, commanding it to stop (see Mark 4:39), and even addressed a corpse, giving it life (see John 11:43). One of His disciples also did this (see Acts 9:36-41).

No, I'm not trying to start a communing-with-nature cult, and I certainly don't believe in communicating with the dead. Neither did Jesus. He knew that nature and dead people weren't hearing Him, but rather that His words were releasing the power of the Holy Spirit to impact these realms.

I believe our words, when they are His words and the Holy Spirit leads us to speak them, also release divine power. That's why I was reading the Bible over a field. Actually, I was reading it over the field and some flies that were invading it. I read the blessings of Deuteronomy 28 concerning the crop: "Blessed shall be . . . the produce of your ground. . . . The Lord will command the blessing . . . in all that you put your hand to, and He will bless you in the land which the Lord your God gives you. . . . And the Lord will make you abound in prosperity . . . in the produce of your ground" (vv. 4,8,11). I read Psalm 91:3 concerning the flies: "For it is He who delivers you from the snare of the trapper, and from the deadly pestilence." The flies died and the crop lived.

The situation was as follows: A Guatemalan farmer, already in financial trouble from previous losses, was in danger of losing thousands of acres of maize to these flies. He was about to spend around $25,000 (US) to have them crop-dusted, and wasn't even sure this would stop the plague. We spoke to this new Christian about the biblical principle of tithing and the promise that God would "rebuke the devourer" (see Mal. 3:10-11) for those who would obey Him in this regard.

We then read to him the verses mentioned above and asked if he would like us to join him in reading and declaring these words of God over his crops. He did, we did, and God did. The crops lived and the flies and their larvae died. The crop-dusting wasn't even necessary. Not only was the crop saved, but so was the $25,000 this would have cost.

Certainly this is a radical example of proclaiming the Word, and some of you may find this odd, yet I've decided it isn't fair to allow the abuses of some to rob others of important and valid truth. When scriptural principles are followed, the spoken Word is a very powerful weapon of intercession.

This information can be taught with accuracy and balance, and we need not get "strange" in applying it. Being balanced biblically does not mean we do nothing that contradicts human understanding or reason. It means we stay in the parameters of biblical teaching and the leading of the Holy Spirit. Much so-called balance in Christianity is simply a desire to stay totally in the realm of our human understanding. This eliminates much of that which requires faith, which certainly includes speaking the Word of God as a weapon.

Jesus not only spoke Holy Spirit-inspired words to a storm and a tree, as mentioned, but when tempted by Satan, the spoken Word of God was His primary weapon against the attack (see Matt. 4:1-11). Ephesians 6:17 calls this "the sword of the Spirit, which is the Word of God." The Greek term translated "word" in this verse means "spoken words," as opposed to written words or unspoken thoughts.[1] The verse, used in this primary New Testament passage on spiritual warfare, is telling us that the Word of God on our lips is a powerful weapon against Satan, as Christ demonstrated.

Why? Because God honors His Word above His very name (see Ps. 138:2, *KJV*). A person's name means nothing if his word can't be trusted. When we look to the Word of God as unfailing and all-powerful, we are giving Him the greatest honor we can give. We're declaring that we know He cannot lie (see Heb. 6:18), that His Word is eternal (see Isa. 40:8), and that He can be trusted implicitly.

A Roman centurion came to Christ on one occasion, asking Him to heal his servant. Christ was willing, and offered to go with the man to minister to his servant. This centurion gave a startling answer, however:

Lord, I am not worthy for You to come under my roof, but just say the word, and my servant will be healed. For I, too, am a man under authority, with soldiers under me; and I say to this one, "Go!" and he goes, and to another, "Come!" and he comes, and to my slave, "Do this!" and he does it (Matt. 8:8-9).

This man understood the authority of God-inspired declarations. Jesus did speak the word, and the servant was healed.

I recall a situation I faced several years ago in which evil spirits were obviously involved. In order to protect the privacy of the individuals involved, I must be vague as to the details, but, generally speaking, great anger, strife and division had arisen in a family. A real possibility existed that this family would be torn apart for years, if not forever.

I prayed late into the night about this very volatile situation, asking God to intervene. After a couple hours of prayer, I heard the Holy Spirit so clearly say, "Speak the Word." The instruction came with such force, I knew it was God talking to me. I began to aggressively declare Scriptures that the Holy Spirit brought to my remembrance, also making commands based upon them, which I felt were appropriate. It went something like this:

- "Behold, I have given you authority to tread upon serpents and scorpions, and over all the power of the enemy, and nothing shall injure you" (Luke 10:19). "Greater is He who is in you than he who is in the world" (1 John 4:4). *I declare that*

God has given me authority over the spirits involved in this situation. The Holy Spirit in me is greater than any power they can muster.

- "For though we walk in the flesh, we do not war after the flesh: For the weapons of our warfare are not carnal, but mighty through God to the pulling down of strongholds casting down imaginations, and every high thing that exalteth itself against the knowledge of God, and bringing into captivity every thought to the obedience of Christ" (2 Cor. 10:3-5, *KJV*). *I declare that my weapons are fully able to disarm this situation. In Jesus' name I tear down the strongholds of the powers of darkness in this family situation.*

- "Submit therefore to God. Resist the devil and he will flee from you" (Jas. 4:7). *I am fully submitted to God and know that as I speak God's Word, the evil forces at work must flee. I command you demonic powers to leave this situation in Jesus' name. I free these individuals from your influence.*

- "If possible, so far as it depends on you, be at peace with all men" (Rom. 12:18). "Honor your father and mother (which is the first commandment with a promise), that it may be well with you, and that you may live long on the earth. And, fathers, do not provoke your children to anger; but bring them up in the discipline and instruction of the Lord" (Eph. 6:2-4). *I declare that*

> *it is God's will that this family be at peace with one*
> *another. I speak these verses as a sword of the Holy*
> *Spirit into this situation to bring peace.*

I probably used some other verses—this was many years ago—but I'm sure you can understand what I was doing. After 10 or 15 minutes of this, I felt great peace in my heart and went to bed. The following morning *every* person involved had a change of heart, and great peace prevailed. The power of God's Word had overcome the evil spirits and positively influenced the minds and hearts of the individuals.

Please notice that I wasn't carrying on a conversation with these spirits, nor was I trying in some extrasensory way to speak to the people involved. I was simply using God's Word as a weapon in the situation, which released the power of the Holy Spirit to prevail and to do what He knew was necessary.

I know of parents who have diligently spoken God's Word over unsaved children in prayer (not in their hearing), using verses such as these:

- God . . . grant them repentance leading them to a knowledge of the truth . . . that they will come to their senses and escape from the trap of the devil, who has taken them captive to do his will (2 Tim. 2:25-26, *NIV*).

- And all thy children shall be taught of the Lord; and great shall be the peace of thy children (Isa. 54:13, *KJV*).

- We have not ceased to pray for you and to ask that you may be filled with the knowledge of His will in all spiritual wisdom and understanding, so that you may walk in a manner worthy of the Lord, to please Him in all respects, bearing fruit in every good work and increasing in the knowledge of God (Col. 1:9-10).

After these parents boldly and diligently declared what the Scriptures state, in time the deceptions and bondages holding the children were broken, and they were saved. I've known others who have done this over marriages, finances, and other things. They simply found Scriptures pertaining to their circumstances and declared them over their situations.

Many years ago, a woman we'll call Stacy (not her real name) experienced a challenging week. The family's business had recently failed, and her husband was on the road as a salesman, trying to generate some income. At home with their five children, she realized there was no money left, and there were only a few groceries in the house. As these supplies dwindled with each meal she served her children, she remembered God's faithfulness. She recalled the story of Elijah and the widow of Zarephath in 1 Kings 17:10-16, and how God had miraculously stretched a handful of flour and a little oil to provide food for many days. She also thought of the seven baskets of leftovers remaining after the apostles had fed four thousand people with the seven loaves of bread and few fish that Jesus had blessed (see Mark 8:1-8).

Stacy prayed that God would also bless their provisions, multiplying them to last as long as necessary. Amazingly, meal after meal, day after day, there was still enough food to satisfy her active children's appetites. Then, at the end of the week, their last meal of the day finally brought an end to the food. As usual, Stacy and the children prayed together at bedtime. She didn't let them know that their food was gone or that there was no money, but she reminded them of Philippians 4:19: "And my God shall supply all your needs according to His riches in glory in Christ Jesus." Together, she and the children asked God to provide what they needed, and thanked Him for doing so.

After tucking them in bed, she went downstairs and sat in her "prayer chair." Opening her Bible to Psalm 37:25, she prayed, "Lord, Your Word says 'I have never seen the righteous forsaken or their children begging bread.' Father, I thank You for the righteousness that we have through Christ Jesus. I believe in Your promise not to forsake us. You care about my children even more than I do. I trust You that they will not have to beg for bread, and that You will provide all that we need."

Startled at that moment by the ringing of her telephone, Stacy went to answer it. It was a long-distance call from a faithful intercessor for her family. "Is everything okay?" the caller asked. "I've been feeling like you could really use some help right now. I just sent $150 to you, and it should be there in the morning." This is a powerful example of how God honors His Word as it is used in intercession.

I am constantly amazed at how many prayer meetings I attend where so little of the Word of God is implemented. The greatest weapon God has given us often goes unsheathed! If Christ, our greatest example, used the spoken Word as His number-one weapon when confronted by Satan himself, shouldn't we use it regularly?

I was impressed recently by one of my daughters' teachers, who sent home to us parents a list of 18 Scriptures to pray over our children. He obviously understands the power of God's Word. Here are a few of the verses:

- Hate evil, you who love the Lord (Ps. 97:10).

- If sinners entice you, do not consent . . . do not walk in the way with them. Keep your feet from their path (Prov. 1:10,15).

- I urge you . . . to present your bodies a living and holy sacrifice, acceptable to God. . . . And do not be conformed to this world, but be transformed by the renewing of your mind, that you may prove what the will of God is, that which is good and acceptable and perfect (Rom. 12:1-2).

- Submit therefore to God. Resist the devil and he will flee from you (Jas. 4:7).

This, I believe, is the highest and most effective level of prayer—praying and declaring the Word of God.

The Hebrew word *asah*, translated "create" in the Genesis story of God creating the world, is also used in the following verses, which are spoken in the context of speaking God's Word:

- God is not a man, that He should lie, nor a son of man, that He should repent. Has He said, and will He not do [*asah*] it? Or has He spoken, and will He not make it good? (Num. 23:19).

- So shall My word be which goes forth from My mouth; it shall not return to Me empty, without accomplishing [*asah*] what I desire, and without succeeding in the matter for which I sent it (Isa. 55:11).

- Then the Lord said to me, "You have seen well, for I am watching over My word to perform [*asah*] it" (Jer. 1:12).

God's Word *does*. God's Word *accomplishes*. God's Word *performs*. In each reference, humans spoke the doing, accomplishing and performing that God's creative Word was going to do! We're obviously not speaking about creating physical matter, but rather creating desired results in human situations.

This leads us to a very important understanding on the subject of declarative intercession. Our declarations must be based on His words, agreeing with Scripture and inspired by the Holy Spirit. The New Testament word for "confession" means literally "to say the same thing as."[2] We are not to walk around thinking that we have the power to command our will into anything and everything. First John 5:14-15 tells us:

And this is the confidence which we have before Him, that, if we ask anything according to His will, He hears us. And if we know that He hears us in whatever we ask, we know that we have the requests which we have asked from Him.

We must find out what the Scriptures teach about our situations and make our biblical confessions and declarations accordingly. We are then saying the same thing He says, which honors Him and gives the Holy Spirit something He can truly empower. This is true biblical declaration and a powerful facet of intercession.

There is, in fact, a wonderful verse in Hebrews 3:1 that says Jesus is the Apostle and High Priest of our confession, which is "saying the same thing" He says. When we speak His words on earth, He can back them up from heaven.

I was ministering recently at a conference in Harlem, New York, when God began to speak to me that He wanted to lift the reproach off of that region and transform it. Known for its violence and poverty, Harlem has an unsavory reputation. Gangs are prevalent, graffiti and trash are everywhere, and drugs, alcohol and perversion seem to rule. Many, many precious, godly people are also there, however, and even those caught in the vicious cycle of past problems are simply victims of a generational life pattern from which they don't know how to break free. Jesus loves them dearly.

In compassion, and under the anointing and inspiration of the Holy Spirit, I stated that God was going to visit Harlem with such revival that it would transform the city and lift the reproach. I then *declared* that God was going to make it a praise in the earth. This is a phrase from Isaiah 62:7.

The following morning a local pastor spoke. In his message this dynamic man of God stated that every Sunday for several years, he and his congregation have declared Isaiah 62:7: "And give Him no rest until He establishes and makes Jerusalem a praise in the earth." They insert the name Harlem for Jerusalem.

I have never spoken this over a city before. Somehow the Holy Spirit in me was able to bring me into agreement with the faith He had put in this congregation. He used me to confirm and agree with their powerful declarations. This blessed and encouraged me, but more important, it was a confirmation to them that their declarations really were motivated and empowered by the Holy Spirit. Harlem will one day be a praise in the earth!

Your city can also be a praise in the earth. So can your life, interceding friend of God!

Down with the flies; up with the harvest!

Let's pray this prayer together:

> *Father, I thank You for Your Word that is a sharp sword and powerful weapon against Satan. I declare Your Word over my children right now. I declare that they will have quick, repentant hearts (see Ps. 51:1-3), that their lives will bear the fruit of the Spirit (see Gal. 5:22-23), that they will trust in You for direction (see Prov. 3:5-6), and that they will live by the Spirit and not gratify their flesh (see Gal. 5:16).* [If you are not praying for children, find applicable Scriptures to declare over the situation or person for which you are praying.] *I ask these things in the name of Jesus, Amen.*

Did You Understand?

1. What did Jesus use as His primary weapon when Satan tempted Him?

2. What does the Hebrew word for "create" (*asah*) have to do with declaring the Word of God?

3. What does the biblical word for "confession" mean? What does this have to do with our High Priest?

4. Are you excited about taking God's Word— your sword—and using it as a powerful weapon and creative force?

Chapter Twelve

The Pain of Intercession

I live in Colorado Springs at the base of Pikes Peak. This majestic mountain towers 14,110 feet and is one of the great tourist attractions in our nation. It was at the top of this incredible mountain peak that Katherine Lee Bates wrote the words to "America the Beautiful."

Thousands of people drive to the pinnacle of this mountain every year to enjoy its panoramic views. Other people—of dubious wisdom, in my opinion—climb it. You don't have to climb it with ropes, spikes, and such—there is a steep trail several miles long that winds its way to the top. I'm told it takes about eight hours to climb—and eight weeks to recover from the PAIN.

I found myself thinking one day that I might try this, but I quickly recovered from this momentary imbalance and promised my spasming body that I would never again think such an insane thought.

I have a friend, Rex Tonkins, who climbed it with his two kids and several other young children. I don't know what possessed him to do this, but we have arranged several weeks of psychiatric care for him. We also agreed not to tell the local social services that he took his kids. Surprisingly, they still love him and want to stay in his care.

He told me that it took them ten and a half hours instead of eight, because the kids had to stop frequently. He ended up carrying their burdens—the packs, water bottles, lunches—most of the way. Serves him right! They should have made him carry them, too.

They're all bragging about it now . . . I think it's the lack of oxygen.

Christ climbed a mountain once. He loaded our "burdens" on His back—sin, sickness, suffering, despair, rejection—tied them to a cross, and carried them to the top. The mountain was called Calvary. Several times He staggered under the weight of our burdens, but love drove Him on to the top.

Isaiah said our sins and other weaknesses were "laid upon" Him (see Isa. 53:6, *KJV*), and He carried them away. The words "laid upon" are translated from *paga*, the Hebrew word for "intercession." This act of substitution was called intercession because one of the meanings of intercession is "to take the place of another."

Of course, that's what we do through intercessory prayer. Acting on behalf of others, we make requests for them. Christ allows us to partake of His priestly ministry of intercession. Just as the Old Testament priests made intercession for Israel, representing that nation to God through their sacrificial system, we represent the needs of others to the Father through the sacrifice of Christ. The Old Testament system was simply a picture of what God planned all along to do in the New Testament or, as the words mean, "new covenant" in Christ.

You also, as living stones, are being built up as a spiritual house for a holy *priesthood*, to offer up *spiritual sacrifices* acceptable to God through Jesus

Christ. For this is contained in Scripture: "Behold I lay in Zion a choice stone, a precious corner stone, and he who believes in Him shall not be disappointed." But you are a chosen race, a royal *priesthood*, a holy nation, a people for God's own possession, that you may proclaim the excellencies of Him who has called you out of darkness into His marvelous light (1 Pet. 2:5-6,9, emphasis added).

I chose to call this chapter the *pain of intercession* because if we allow the Holy Spirit to help us walk in this ministry to the fullest, it can be spiritually and emotionally painful. We bear one another's weaknesses—not in the sense that Christ did, but we carry them in prayer. Consider the following verses:

Now we who are strong ought to bear the weaknesses of those without strength and not just please ourselves. Let each of us please his neighbor for his good, to his edification (Rom. 15:1-2).

Bear one another's burdens, and thus fulfill the law of Christ (Gal. 6:2).

And if one member suffers, all the members suffer with it; if one member is honored, all the members rejoice with it (1 Cor. 12:26).

Dick Eastman shares a remarkable incident in his life that illustrates the extent to which God can allow us to move into this precious, priestly aspect of Christ's intercession.

Several years ago, Dick was interceding for 153 children who were being held hostage by terrorists in Holland. The news media provided day-to-day coverage of this situation, and one day, as the terrorists' demands intensified, the Lord brought him to an entirely different level of intercession.

While praying in his backyard prayer chapel, Eastman suddenly could see himself inside the schoolhouse where the children were being held. As he looked at them through his spiritual eyes, he was startled to recognize his own six- and nine-year-old daughters among those held captive. He knew his girls were actually sleeping in the house just a few feet away, but this mental picture caused him to enter into the intercessor's role of identification as the Holy Spirit laid upon him an intensity of prayer like none he had ever experienced.

Trembling with indignation, he authoritatively commanded the terrorists to let the children go. Various emotions exuded from him as he, from the position of being a parent of these children, labored in intercession over them, demanding their release. Sensing victory, the time of intercession abruptly ended. He went to the office a few minutes later and didn't give it another thought throughout the day.

That evening, while at the family dinner table, he happened to see out of the corner of his eye a television left on in the family room. Catching his attention was a news report that three of the Dutch children had been released. Rather than being thrilled with this victory, Eastman was surprised to find his eyes filling with tears. *Jesus,* he said in his heart, *I didn't ask for three children; I asked for all of them to be released. And that was a prayer born of Your Spirit.* With a fresh burst of boldness, he pounded the table with his fist and declared, "And I claim the miracle now!"

At the exact moment he hit the table, a local reporter interrupted the news broadcast to clarify that the report just aired had been recorded earlier and was incomplete. He went on to inform the viewers that actually all 153 children had been freed early that morning.

Eastman's amazement at the precise timing of this continues to this day. He knew beyond a doubt that his prayers had made a difference, as had those of other believers. This incredible experience will always be a vivid reminder to him of how God can use the power of identification to impact the lives of others through intercession.[1]

That is *paga!* Oh, the sweet, sweet pain of intercession. Our union with Christ, who is still "touched with the feeling of our infirmities" (Heb. 4:15, *KJV*), is what makes such identification with the problems and difficulties of others possible. First Corinthians 6:17 tells us, "But the one who joins himself to the Lord is one spirit with Him." Second Peter 1:4 states that we are "partakers of the divine nature," and that nature includes a heart of great compassion.

Jesus was often moved with compassion (see Matt. 9:36-38; 14:14; 15:32; and others) and has "poured out within our hearts through the Holy Spirit" this same love (Rom. 5:5). We are to be people of love, filled with the compassion of Christ, living not just for ourselves, but accepting the privilege of extending His love on the earth. To do this effectively, we must allow Him to *truly* love through us, moving us with His compassion.

Eastman expresses this beautifully as he defines compassion in his book *Love on Its Knees*.

> *Compassion* is derived from the two Latin words *com* and *pati*, *com* meaning "with" or "together" and *pati* meaning "to suffer" or "to hurt." Combined, these expressions describe one who "*suffers with*" someone in need or "*hurts together*" with those experiencing pain.
>
> Compassion is more than mere pity. It is love in its dynamic phase, love released through action. It is a life of involvement in the struggles of others. Christ gave us the fullest expression of active compassion when He went to the cross to remove the suffering brought on humankind through sin. Jesus was not an intercessor just when He prayed, as we have already seen; He lived the life of intercession. Jesus is compassion. When He prayed, it was compassion praying. To see Christ in prayer is to see Love on its knees.[2]

I recently attended The Call D.C. As mentioned in chapter 10, this was a gathering of four hundred thousand youth and adults (mostly youth) on the Washington Mall in our nation's capital for the purpose of repenting, fasting and praying for revival in America. I, along with many others, believe revival is coming to America, and that the youth are to play a major role. This is one of the reasons many leaders in America believe this gathering was so crucial. I believe it was one of the most important days in the history of our nation.

At one point in the day, as I was in a time of extreme repentance for the sins of my generation against the younger generation, I began to feel the deep pain of the Holy Spirit regarding these sins. As I repented over abortion, abandonment, abuse, sexual impurity, and addiction, all things we have done to or passed on to their generation, I thought at one point my heart was going to break. (Even as I write this, I'm beginning to feel the grief again.) I sobbed from so deep within, my stomach was heaving. I was feeling their pain, the Father's broken heart, and my generation's shame. It was nearly unbearable. I was physically and emotionally undone.

This was the pain of intercession. The burden I felt was being "laid upon" me by the Holy Spirit for the purpose of intercession. Mercifully, it lifted after a short season, though I still carry it to a lesser degree.

John G. Lake, a man used mightily in Africa in the early 1900s, exemplifies this love and its *paga* release of power.

Lake was asked to pray for the bedridden wife of a government official. When he visited this woman, a believer, he gave her Scriptures to study to activate her faith for healing from the terminal cancer. Deciding to trust God for her healing, she also determined not to take any further medication. The doctors had been giving her pain relievers to ease her discomfort while awaiting her death. After stopping this medication, her pain became so intense that Lake and another minister stayed at her side continuously, as she would experience some relief when they prayed.

One morning, after going home briefly, Lake was two blocks away from her house when he heard her screams of pain. Without realizing what he was doing, he ran to her side and took her into his arms. As he held her and wept, she was completely healed. What a powerful testimony of the compassion of Jesus, the love of God, permeating a person in close fellowship with Him, allowing healing to come to another![3]

I found myself touched recently by Christ's love for the Muslim world. While in prayer with a group of intercessors with whom I pray regularly, the Holy Spirit began to move upon us. His heart for those precious people who are caught in the maze of Islamic deception was imparted to us. We interceded—"taking the place of another"—fervently for them.

Pertinent to this, Sam Brassfield, my dear friend and one of my spiritual fathers, had told me for several years that he believed God would one day use me to penetrate some of the Arab nations with the gospel. I had believed and accepted this, though the "burden" of the Lord had not yet been imparted to me on their behalf.

Please don't misunderstand this. I had cared about them, prayed for them, and given money to reach them. But God had not yet put into my heart what I knew would one day come to me—His all-consuming, passionate love that transforms a concern into a burden. Pain of heart! The kind of love Paul said constrained (made a "prisoner" of) him (see 2 Cor. 5:14, *KJV*). It simply wasn't time.

This began, however, in that *paga* meeting. Tears flowed, we cried out with great passion and holy love, and my life began to change. The Spirit of Christ began to penetrate my heart, as well as the hearts of those praying with me. Intercession flowed as we cried out for their salvation. *The pain of intercession*!

After this went on for a while, the Holy Spirit clearly spoke to my heart, telling me to have my book *Intercessory Prayer* translated into Arabic. We quickly picked up a copy of the book, placed it in front of us, and laid our hands on it as the intercession continued. Again, the tears flowed and streams of intercession poured forth as this burden was "laid upon" us. I have now begun to raise the necessary funds to do this, and have no doubt that I will be used in other ways to reach the Muslim world.

That is the compassion of Christ, resulting in the burden of the Lord being carried and released . . . *paga* . . . intercession.

Paul experienced this for the Jews in Romans 9:1-3 when he said:

I am telling the truth in Christ, I am not lying, my conscience bearing me witness in the Holy Spirit, that I have *great sorrow* and *unceasing grief* in my heart. For I could wish that I myself were accursed, separated from Christ for the sake of my brethren, my kinsmen according to the flesh (emphasis added).

More than human compassion, this was the love of the great High Priest in heaven flowing through one of his representative priests on Earth. Epaphras experienced it for the believers in Colossae, who were being led into deception:

Epaphras, who is one of your number, a bondslave of Jesus Christ, sends you his greetings, always *laboring earnestly* for you in his prayers, that you may stand perfect and fully assured in all the will of God. For I bear him witness that he has a *deep concern* for you (Col. 4:12-13, emphasis added).

Again, this is Christ's love flowing through a person for the purpose of intercession—"taking the place of another"—in prayer.

Jesus, while ministering in His earthly body, was overcome with compassion for Lazarus and his two sisters, Mary and Martha. He wept in intercession for them, until his *paga* released so much divine power that resurrection life flowed into Lazarus' dark tomb and filled his dead body with new life (see John 11:35-44). He now wants to release that compassion and life force through us. We are His hands and feet, and the expressers of His great love. We're His representatives on Earth, through whom He desires to release spiritual resurrection power.

The following story is told of Francis of Assisi and how his life was drastically altered:

Born into a wealthy Italian family, Francesco de Pietro Berardone seemed headed for a life of abundance. However, all that changed one afternoon in a transforming moment while he rode his pony around the city. Turning a corner, the pony abruptly halted, and Francesco was shocked by the sight in front of him. A leper, with his body partially eaten away by the disease, stood in the path. Sickened by the man's appearance, Francesco turned away and was about to return home.

But the Spirit of God suddenly opened Francesco's eyes to eternal realities, and, as he looked again at the leper, he recognized his own spiritually depraved condition as being worse than the dying man's leprosy. He leapt from his pony, embraced the leper, and gently kissed the suffering man as he gave him his bag of gold. Francesco had been baptized with the compassion of Christ, and his life would never be the same. He surrendered to his Savior outside the city of Assisi, and continued his life of compassion, becoming one of history's most remarkable spiritual warriors.[4]

Francis of Assisi was a human like you and me. Yet he allowed the great Lover of the universe to penetrate his human soul. He was introduced to the pain of intercession, as the burden of this pitiful leper was laid upon him. Lake, Eastman, Paul, and every other human who has been mightily used by God in this high calling of intercession have allowed the same. You can, too.

Millions of spiritual lepers are waiting for someone to touch them with God's love. We must leap from our comfortable "ponies" and fall to our knees, allowing the compassion of Christ to become ours. He wants to kiss suffering humanity with His healing lips.

I must warn you, this is a costly ministry. A superficial, casual attempt at caring will not be acceptable to God. He is looking for those who will truly care. He actually prefers cold indifference to half-hearted hypocrisy (see Rev. 3:15-16).

If you allow Christ to touch you with His passionate heart, it will make you a prisoner of love. Your life will change: attitudes, lifestyle, the spending of time and money, what you find yourself thinking about, goals and plans—everything will change.

Yet the benefits will far outweigh the pain. You'll become a life changer and a history maker. You'll partner with the greatest Lover the world has ever known. He will look through your eyes, hear through your ears, touch through your hands, and love through your broken but fulfilled heart. The pain of intercession will become the pleasure of intercession.

Climb the mountain with Christ! You can make it to the top! Take up your cross, allow the burdens of others to be placed upon you, and carry them to the Father. He will meet with you, meet with them, and the power of the cross will be released.

Maybe I'll climb Pikes Peak after all.

Let's pray this prayer together:

Father, I want to be touched by Your heart.
Help me to feel Your love for Susan [insert the name
of the person for whom you're praying]. *Your Word
says, "If one member suffers, all the members suffer
with it." I am willing to have this burden laid upon me
that I might pray with Your compassion.*
*Please touch her hurting heart, Father, and bring Your
peace to her in the midst of this storm. Give her great
grace as she leans on You for strength. Make very real
to her the promise that she can cast all of her cares upon
You because You love her so much.*
In Christ's authority I ask this,
Amen.

Did You Understand?

1. What is meant by "the pain of intercession"?

2. Give and comment on some verses that instruct
   us to bear one another's burdens.

3. How is it possible for us to receive Christ's
   compassion?

4. Are you willing to climb the mountain?

Chapter Thirteen

The Pleasure of Intercession

I love to spend time in the woods. Sitting, walking, standing—it really doesn't matter much—I just love to be there. God and I have spent hundreds, probably thousands, of hours enjoying one another in these quiet "Hebrons."

I recall one such occasion. I was walking quietly, inwardly worshiping along with peaceful praise music on my Walkman. It seemed on this occasion, as it has on many others, that I had walked right into God's very presence. We were truly walking together.

As I rounded a curve in the trail and topped a small rise, I came face to face with three deer. I immediately stopped, not wanting to startle them, and they glanced at me without alarm and went on with their peaceful browsing. It was like a moment frozen in time for me.

The instant I stopped, the chorus "In Moments Like These" began to play on my Walkman. I stood frozen, listening to this worship chorus, savoring my God-given moment with Him. As I quietly worshiped Him, enjoying His company and the scene He had so graciously prepared for me, I realized how special it was for Him, too.

The deer? They simply glanced at me once in a while as if to say, "It's okay. We know Him, too."

I've had many such encounters with God—in woods, cars, prayer rooms, even in crowded malls. I can hardly wait for the next one. In this chapter on *the pleasure of intercession*, I want to bring you back to where we started: the joy of partnering with your Father and Friend.

I asked some friends to help me by sharing with you their thoughts on the pleasure of intercession. I think you'll be blessed and inspired by what they have to say.

Timmerle DeKeyser, a friend and a personal intercessor for me and my family, as well as the minister of prayer at the church I pastor, had this to say:

> To me, intercession is just like serving a King. I may be summoned to His presence at any hour of the day or night. When I answer this call to come into His court, He then shares with me the secret burdens on His heart, and I find myself weeping with Him. What an awesome privilege to commune heart to heart with the King of kings! Knowing Him in this place of intimacy is a treasure that cannot be measured.
>
> Sometimes, I feel my heart burn with His anger at an unjust situation, and I have also felt the overwhelming joy of victory when He has trounced His enemies.
>
> But the greatest pleasure of all is knowing the depth of His love. As I pray and lift up others before His throne of grace, I feel an intensity of love that is beyond my own comprehension, as the way He loves each one is somehow imparted to me.
>
> Now and then, overwhelmed with a deep sense of awe, I lie on the floor for hours before Him. Unable to speak, perhaps softly weeping, I feel a

depth of love that is impossible to describe to others. *God is love.*

I believe this is His reward for us, His intercessors: He brings us into such an amazing depth of His presence that it is hard for us to leave that place. It's like a little sneak preview of Revelation 4 and 5. How could I live any other way? I'm spoiled for the ordinary. I'm in love with a King.

Powerful, isn't it? That kind of intimacy is available to you, as well. Another of my personal intercessors, Julie Whitney, shared the following:

One of the pleasures of intercession that thrills my heart is the realm of intimacy it creates in my relationship with the Lord. It's a two-way line of communication: back and forth. A picture the Lord once showed me was of the two of us meeting at a little café table in Paris, France. I often remember this in times of prayer. We sit together at this table, facing one another. He will then speak into my ear what He wants me to intercede for, call forth, or decree, and I do it. He may speak to me about a person, church, nation or situation. It's not just me voicing my own agenda, but rather an intimate conversation between the two of us.

The Lord wants to reveal to us His intimate secrets and what is on His heart to accomplish. With purpose, intent and authority, we then declare what we have heard Him say.

A certain phrase in a song says, "When I find the joy of reaching Your heart." One of the pleasures of intercession is reaching the Lord's heart and praying it.

The pleasure of intercession is being in the presence of the Lord. And as I am in His presence, I am changed and conformed to His image. I see the word "please" in the word "pleasure." The pleasure in intercession is that we please the Lord by co-laboring with Him. Psalm 103:21 states, "Bless ye the Lord, all ye his heavenly hosts; ye ministers of His, that do His pleasure" (*KJV*).

Julie is a powerful intercessor and, as you can tell, her power flows from intimacy with the Father.

Judy Ball is also an intercessor used greatly of the Lord. While a mighty warrior, she, too, knows the pleasure of intercession:

The Word of God is true. The work of intercession, through the Body of Christ on Earth, taps the power in heaven to do the greater works of Jesus. I take great joy in knowing that in every tribe, tongue and language (see Rev. 7:9) there are brothers and sisters who are interceding through the guidance of the Holy Spirit. I am a small part of that greater work of power released through prayer.

I find great pleasure in being the vessel that brings about this meeting between heaven and Earth. Great humility, joy and awe follow such experiences. The pleasure of intercession becomes great fulfillment as family, friends, leaders and nations are benefited.

The realization that, as an intercessor in Christ, I can touch the heart of our Father in heaven brings great pleasure. As I pray His heart, many things are accomplished that otherwise would not occur. The key to this happening is being obedient to listen and obey while sacrificing my entire being to pray "Thy kingdom come, Thy will be done." Intercession has become living persistently in the presence of God. "In His presence is fullness of joy" (Ps. 16:11).

Bobbye Byerly is a dear friend and personal intercessor of mine. She embodies prayer. I see Jesus on her countenance and hear Him in her voice. Only heaven knows the incredible fruit of her life as an intercessor.

The pleasure of His presence is my greatest joy and highest reward. I have been an intercessor since 1970. One day our pastor stopped me and said, "Bobbye, God has shown me He has gifted you with the ministry of intercession. Would you pray for me daily?"

I looked at him and said, "What is intercession?" As he began to explain I said, "Oh, that is how I enjoy God's presence. I did not know there was a name for it."

I have spent more time in my secret chamber than any other place. I just love meeting with

God. I am under His orders to discharge His purposes according to His management. At times, I feel like Isaiah when he said, "Also I heard the voice of the Lord, saying, 'Whom shall I send, and who will go for us?' Then I said, 'Here am I! Send me.'"

What a privilege to express a few of my deep longings for the God of the whole universe! How tenderly He leans over heaven's balcony and draws us to Himself. May God continue to woo us into His presence. Those who walk in the fear of the Lord will know their God, and He will reveal His secrets and His mysteries to His friends (intercessors) who keep His covenant.

The true pleasure of intercession is when the recognition of Jesus in our lives causes others to meet with God, as shared by Quin Sherrer in her book *Good Night, Lord*:

That Sunday night, in an unplanned good-bye, the pastor let her address our congregation from the microphone. She was just thirteen.

"I've been here in the detention home for some months now," she admitted. "But on weekends I've been allowed to visit in some of your homes. You've fed me, clothed me, and, best of all, you have introduced me to Jesus. I'm rehabilitated now and ready to return to my own town—my own home. But I'm so thrilled with what Jesus has done for me, I want to thank Him."

She raised a finger and pointed out at the audience. "While I want to thank Jesus, I remember that you are Him here, so I will thank you." There was hardly a dry eye in the sanctuary as she continued pointing her tiny finger at various ones who had exhibited the love of Jesus to her in practical ways.

Home. She was going home. That had two meanings now: a real home with parents and, someday, an eternal home with her heavenly Father.

After her public good-bye, our pastor had dozens of plaques made, for any family in the church who wanted one. The plaque was inscribed with the words: "You are Him here." Many of us hung them in our homes as a reminder that we are Christ's representatives to anyone who enters our home.

Teresa of Avila, a sixteenth-century nun, wrote, "Christ has no hands on earth but yours. No feet on earth but yours, no eyes of compassion on earth but yours. He has no body on earth but yours."

You are Him here![1]

Yes, you are. Enjoy it. Many wonderful moments await you as you partner with Him. Testimonies will be written, destinies will be shaped, and eternity will be different for many because you discovered the pleasure of intercession.

Enjoy the journey!

Endnotes

Chapter One: The Priority of Intercession

1. Craig Brian Larson, *Contemporary Illustrations for Preachers, Teachers and Writers* (Grand Rapids, MI: Baker, 1996), p. 70.
2. Alice Gray, *Stories for a Faithful Heart* (Portland, OR: Multnomah, 2000), adapted from pp. 69-70.
3. Pauline Youd, *Decision*, March 1992, p. 39.
4. Ken Gaub, *God's Got Your Number* (Kingwood, TX: Hunter Books, 1984), adapted from pp. 83-84.
5. Quin Sherrer and Ruthanne Garlock, *How to Pray for Your Family and Friends* (Ann Arbor, MI: Servant, 1990), adapted from pp. 67-68.
6. Story forwarded by emails from several sources.

Chapter Two: The Plan of Intercession

1. As quoted in Paul E. Billheimer, *Destined for the Throne* (Fort Washington, PA: Christian Literature Crusade, 1975), p. 51.
2. C. Peter Wagner, *Confronting the Powers* (Ventura, CA: Regal, 1996), p. 242.
3. Jack Canfield, Mark Victor Hansen, Patty Aubery and Nancy Mitchell Autio, *Chicken Soup for the Christian Family Soul* (Deerfield Beach, FL: Health Communications, 2000), adapted from pp. 64–67.
4. Hebrew word: *mashal.*
5. Hebrew word: *nathan.*
6. Hebrew word: *shamar.*
7. Quinn Sherrer and Ruthanne Garlock, *How to Pray for Your Family and Friends* (Ann Arbor, MI: Servant, 1990), pp. 58-59.

Chapter Three: The Person of Intercession

1. Greek word: *tetelestai.*
2. Greek word: *luo.*

Chapter Four: The Purpose of Intercession

1. Greek word: *pro-orizo.*
2. Francis Brown, S. R. Driver, and Charles A. Briggs, *The New Brown-Driver, Briggs-Gesenius Hebrew and English Lexicon* (Peabody, MA: Hendrickson, 1979), p. 803.
3. Adapted from Gary Lane, "Revival in Ethiopia," as displayed on internet newsstand www.700club.org in October 1999.
4. *The Consolidated Webster Encyclopedic Dictionary* (Chicago: Consolidated, 1954), p. 384.
5. Gordon Lindsay, *25 Objectives to Divine Healing and the Bible Answers* (Dallas, TX: Christ For the Nations, 1973), 31, 32.
6. Alice Gray, *Stories for a Faithful Heart* (Portland, OR: Multnomah, 2000), adapted from pp. 207–211.

Chapter Five: The Prize of Intercession

1. R. A. Torrey, *How to Pray* (Springdale, PA: Whitaker House, 1983), p. 20.
2. Oswald J. Smith, *The Passion for Souls* (Burlington, ON: Welch, 1984), p. 33.
3. Dick Eastman, *Love on Its Knees* (Tarrytown, NY: Chosen, 1989), adapted from p. 18.
4. Ibid., adapted from pp. 18-19.
5. Greek word: *kalupsis* is "veil"; *apokalupsis* is "revelation."
6. Charles G. Finney, *Revival Lectures* (Old Tappan, NJ: Fleming H. Revell, n.d.), pp. 99-100.
7. Greek word: *hupsoma*.
8. Kenneth E. Hagin, *The Art of Intercession* (Tulsa, OK: Rhema Bible Church, 1980), p. 47.
9. Greek word: *noema*.
10. Quin Sherrer and Ruthanne Garlock, *A Woman's Guide to Spiritual Warfare* (Ann Arbor, MI: Servant, 1991), adapted from pp. 45-46.
11. Hebrew word: *rachaph*.
12. Clarence W. Hall, *Miracle in Cannibal Country* (Costa Mesa, CA: Gift Publications, 1980), adapted from pp. 19-21.

Chapter Six: The Place of Intercession

1. Ken Gaub, *God's Got Your Number* (Kingwood, TX: Hunter Books, 1984), adapted from pp. 1–10.
2. Edward K. Rowell, *Fresh Illustrations for Preaching and Teaching* (Grand Rapids, MI: Baker, 1997), p. 165.
3. Thetus Tenney, *Prayer Takes Wings* (Ventura, CA: Renew, 2000), adapted from p. 92.

Chapter Seven: The Protection of Intercession

1. Dick Eastman and Jack Hayford, *Living and Praying in Jesus' Name* (Wheaton, IL: Tyndale, 1988), p. 52.
2. Ibid., adapted from pp. 13–14.
3. Gordon Lindsay, *Prayer That Moves Mountains* (Dallas, TX: Christ For the Nations, revised 1994), adapted from p. 39.
4. Greek word: *kairos*.
5. Hebrew word: *eth*.
6. Oral Roberts, *A Prayer Cover over Your Life* (Tulsa, OK: Oral Roberts, 1990), adapted from pp. 10–11.
7. Quin Sherrer, *Listen, God Is Speaking to You* (Ann Arbor, MI: Servant, 1999), pp. 148-149.
8. Eastman and Hayford, p. 129.
9. *The International Standard Bible Encyclopedia*, (Grand Rapids, MI: Eerdmans, 1986), 4:964.
10. E. M. Bounds, *The Necessity of Prayer* (Springdale, PA Whitaker House, 1984), p. 7.

Chapter Eight: The Power of Intercession

1. Jane Rumph, *Stories from the Front Lines* (Grand Rapids MI: Chosen, 1996), adapted from pp. 187–191.

2. Dutch Sheets, *Intercessory Prayer* (Ventura, CA: Regal, 1996), p. 180.

3. Dudley Hall, *Incense and Thunder* (Sisters, OR: Multnomah, 1999), p. 27.

4. Esther Ilnisky, *Let the Children Pray* (Ventura, CA: Regal, 2000), pp. 103-104.

5. Greek word: *mega*.

6. C. Peter Wagner, *Blazing the Way* (Ventura, CA: Regal, 1995), pp. 165-166.

7. Rumph, p. 180.

8. Ibid., adapted from pp. 181-185.

9. Greek word: *anaideia*.

10. Greek word: *sunantilambanomai*.

11. Kenneth E. Hagin, *The Art of Intercession* (Tulsa, OK: Rhema Bible Church, 1980), adapted from p. 29.

12. I also believe this to include praying in tongues.

13. *New Webster's Dictionary and Thesaurus of the English Language* (New York: Lexicon, 1991), s.v. "synergism."

14. Greek word: *sunergos*.

15. Gordon Lindsay, *Prayer That Moves Mountains* (Dallas, TX: Christ For the Nations, revised 1994), adapted from p. 67.

Chapter Nine: The Perseverance of Intercession

1. George Müller, *Release the Power of Prayer* (New Kensington, PA: Whitaker House, 1999), p. 143.

2. Craig Brian Larson, *Choice Contemporary Stories and Illustrations* (Grand Rapids, MI: Baker, 1998), p. 204.

3. Greek word: *chronos*.

4. Greek word: *kairos*.

5. Greek word: *pleroo*.

6. Larson, *Choice Contemporary Stories and Illustrations*, p. 169.

7. Paul E. Billheimer, *Destined for the Throne* (Fort Washington, PA: Christian Literature Crusade, 1975), p. 107.

8. Jane Rumph, *Stories From the Front Lines* (Grand Rapids MI: Chosen, 1996), adapted from pp. 33-35.

9. Gordon Lindsay, *Prayer That Moves Mountains* (Dallas, TX: Christ For the Nations, revised 1994), adapted from pp. 104-105.

10. S. D. Gordon, *What It Will Take to Change the World* (Grand Rapids, MI: Baker, 1979), adapted from pp. 42-45.

Chapter Ten: Proactive Intercession

1. I cover this topic in great detail in my book *Watchman Prayer* (Ventura, CA: Regal, 2000).

2. Hebrew words: *natsar; shamar; tsaphah*.

3. Greek words: *gregoreuo; agrupneo*.

4. Greek word: *agnoeo*.

5. Greek word: *noema*.

6. Greek word: *pleonekteo*.

7. Sheets, *Watchman Prayer*, pp. 19-20.

8. Edward K. Rowell, *Fresh Illustrations for Preaching and Teaching* (Grand Rapids, MI: Baker, 1997), p. 146.

9. Eddie Smith, *Help! I'm Married to an Intercessor* (Ventura, CA: Renew, 1998), pp. 35-36.
10. Elmer L. Towns, *Praying the Lord's Prayer for Spiritual Breakthrough* (Ventura, CA: Regal, 1997), adapted from p. 184.
11. Cindy Jacobs, *The Voice of God* (Ventura, CA: Regal, 1995), pp. 176–78.
12. Elizabeth Alves, *Becoming a Prayer Warrior* (Ventura, CA: Renew, 1998), pp. 29- 30.

Chapter Eleven: Proclamation Intercession
1. Greek word: *rhema*.
2. Greek word: *homologia*.

Chapter Twelve: The Pain of Intercession
1. Dick Eastman, *Love on Its Knees* (Tarrytown, NY: Chosen, 1989), adapted from pp. 35–37.
2. Ibid., p. 28.
3. Kenneth E. Hagin, *The Art of Intercession* (Tulsa, OK: Rhema Bible Church, 1980), adapted from pp. 42-43.
4. Eastman, *Love on Its Knees* , adapted from pp. 26-27.

Chapter Thirteen: The Pleasure of Intercession
1. Quin Sherrer, *Good Night, Lord* (Ventura, CA: Regal, 2000), p. 193.

Bibliography

Alves, Elizabeth. *Becoming a Prayer Warrior*. Ventura, CA: Renew, 1998.

Billheimer, Paul E. *Destined for the Throne*. Fort Washington, PA: Christian Literature Crusade, 1975.

Bounds, E. M. *The Necessity of Prayer*. Springdale, PA: Whitaker House, 1984.

Brown, Francis, S. R. Driver and Charles A. Briggs. *The New Brown-Driver, Briggs-Gesenius Hebrew and English Lexicon*. Peabody, MA: Hendrickson, 1979.

Canfield, Jack, Mark Victor Hansen, Patty Aubery and Nancy Mitchell Autio. *Chicken Soup for the Christian Family Soul*. Deerfield Beach, FL: Health Communications, 2000.

The Consolidated Webster Encyclopedic Dictionary. Chicago: Consolidated, 1954.

Eastman, Dick. *Love on Its Knees*. Tarrytown, NY: Chosen, 1989.

Eastman, Dick, and Jack Hayford. *Living and Praying in Jesus' Name*. Wheaton, IL: Tyndale, 1988.

Finney, Charles G. *Revival Lectures*. Old Tappan, NJ: Fleming H. Revell, n.d..

Gaub, Ken. *God's Got Your Number*. Kingwood, TX: Hunter Books, 1984.

Gordon, S. D. *What It Will Take to Change the World*. Grand Rapids, MI: Baker, 1979.

Gray, Alice. *Stories for a Faithful Heart*. Portland, OR: Multnomah, 2000.

Hagin, Kenneth E. *The Art of Intercession*. Tulsa, OK: Rhema Bible Church, 1980.

Hall, Clarence W. *Miracle in Cannibal Country*. Costa Mesa, CA: Gift Publications, 1980.

Hall, Dudley. *Incense and Thunder*. Sisters, OR: Multnomah, 1999.

Ilnisky, Esther. *Let the Children Pray*. Ventura, CA: Regal, 2000.

The International Standard Bible Encyclopedia, vol. 4. Grand Rapids, MI: Eerdmans, 1986.

Jacobs, Cindy. *The Voice of God*. Ventura, CA: Regal, 1995.

Larson, Craig Brian. *Choice Contemporary Stories and Illustrations*. Grand Rapids, MI: Baker, 1998.

———. *Contemporary Illustrations for Preachers, Teachers and Writers*. Grand Rapids, MI: Baker, 1996.

Lindsay, Gordon. *Prayer That Moves Mountains*. Dallas, TX: Christ For the Nations, revised 1994.

———. *25 Objectives to Divine Healing and the Bible Answers*. Dallas, TX: Christ For the Nations, 1973.

Muller, George. *Release the Power of Prayer*. New Kensington, PA: Whitaker House, 1999.

New Webster's Dictionary and Thesaurus of the English Language. New York: Lexicon, 1991.

Roberts, Oral. *A Prayer Cover over Your Life*. Tulsa, OK: Oral Roberts, 1990.

Rowell, Edward K. *Fresh Illustrations for Preaching and Teaching*. Grand Rapids, MI: Baker, 1997.

Rumph, Jane. *Stories from the Front Lines*. Grand Rapids, MI: Chosen, 1996.

Sheets, Dutch. *Intercessory Prayer*. Ventura, CA: Regal, 1996.

———. *Watchman Prayer*. Ventura, CA: Regal, 2000.

Sherrer, Quin. *Good Night, Lord*. Ventura, CA: Regal, 2000.

———. *Listen, God Is Speaking to You*. Ann Arbor, MI: Servant, 1999.

Sherrer, Quin, and Ruthanne Garlock. *A Woman's Guide to Spiritual Warfare*. Ann Arbor, MI: Servant, 1991.

———. *How to Pray for Your Family and Friends*. Ann Arbor, MI: Servant, 1990.

Smith, Eddie. *Help! I'm Married to an Intercessor*. Ventura, CA: Renew, 1998.

Smith, Oswald J. *The Passion for Souls*. Burlington, ON: Welch, 1984.

Tenney, Thetus. *Prayer Takes Wings*. Ventura, CA: Renew, 2000.

Torrey, R. A. *How to Pray*. Springdale, PA: Whitaker House, 1983.

Towns, Elmer L. *Praying the Lord's Prayer for Spiritual Breakthrough*. Ventura, CA: Regal, 1997.

Wagner, C. Peter. *Blazing the Way*. Ventura, CA: Regal, 1995.

———. *Confronting the Powers*. Ventura, CA: Regal, 1996.

3945 North Academy Boulevard
Colorado Springs, CO 80917
(719) 548- 8226
Fax (719) 548- 8793

Becoming Who You Are

This CD and DVD in-depth study of the soul of man
looks at why most Christians never become all they
are declared to be in Jesus Christ.

Discover Your Destiny

This CD in-depth, yet practical, series will enable you
to discover and fulfill your God-given destiny.

Intercessory Prayer—
The Lightning of God

This CD and DVD series is an in-depth study of the
biblical principles of intercessory prayer.

Unleash the Power of Prayer

This CD series provide in-depth teaching on how our
prayers release God's power as we partner with Him.

More Great Resources from Regal

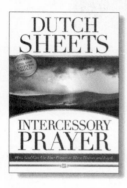

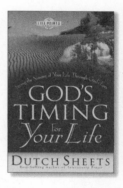